The
Story of Life Insurance

BY

BURTON J. HENDRICK

NEW YORK
McCLURE, PHILLIPS & CO.
MCMVII

PUBLISHER'S NOTE

THE following articles were undertaken at the request of the editors of *McClure's Magazine*, in which periodical they were first published. They represent an attempt to describe, in clear and accurate terms, the causes that led to the insurance scandals of 1905-06. Necessarily such an exposition took historical form, for the evils disclosed by the Armstrong Investigating Committee had existed for many years. Necessarily also, any adequate explanation involved a discussion of life-insurance principles, for it was the abandonment and perversion of sound life-insurance ideas that made possible the dishonest and extravagant use of life-insurance funds. The articles are republished in book form, practically as written, because they have been generally accepted, by both the professional and non-professional reader, as the most successful attempt made to elucidate a difficult subject, and because it is believed that they contain a large amount of historical material which has permanent value and which is unobtainable in any other form.

CONTENTS

CHAPTER   PAGE

I. The Surplus the Basis of Corruption . . 3

II. The Pioneer 51

III. The "Founder" of the Equitable . . . 92

IV. The Great Combine Gamble 129

V. The Thirty Years' War 170

VI. The Raid on the Surplus 209

VII. The Race for Bigness 254

LIST OF ILLUSTRATIONS

ELIZUR WRIGHT . . . . *Frontispiece*

Facing page

ELIZUR WRIGHT IN 1844 54

HENRY B. HYDE AT 22 92

HENRY HAZEN HYDE 94

JOHN C. JOHNSTON 96

FREDERICK S. WINSTON 96

JOSEPH B. COLLINS 96

HENRY B. HYDE IN 1868 132

AMZI DODD 190

JACOB L. GREENE 194

CHAPTER I

THE SURPLUS THE BASIS OF CORRUPTION

FOR the last thirty-five years a constant warfare has been fought in the United States between the good and the bad in life insurance. On one side have ranged honesty, economy, and fair and liberal treatment of the insured; on the other, dishonesty, extravagance, and absolute disregard of policy-holders' rights. Certain companies have treated life insurance as a great beneficent institution, organised for the purpose of protecting the weak and the dependent against adverse fortune; others have regarded it largely as a convenient contrivance for enriching the few men who happened to have usurped control.

In this thirty-five years the history of American life insurance has been one of progressive degeneration. The people have forgotten the old ideals; have persistently abandoned good life insurance and taken up with bad. They have for the larger part ignored the teachings of our great American leaders—men like Elizur Wright, of Massachusetts, the originator of nearly everything that is best in the American system,

Jacob L. Greene, of Hartford, and Amzi Dodd, of New Jersey; and have sought the leadership of men who have degraded the whole institution. They have thus displaced the United States from the world leadership in life insurance which it formerly held, and have made what was one of our greatest claims to national distinction the cause of what is, in many ways, our most shameful national scandal.

To show this deterioration in quality we need not necessarily look far. The most popular companies, indeed, have largely ceased to do a life-insurance business at all. If you study the literature they circulate, you will find the life-insurance feature of their contracts only incidentally mentioned. They talk little about protection of one's family, but much about savings banks, investments, guaranteed incomes, five per cent. Consols, and gold bonds. They ask you to buy their policies, not that thereby you may provide financial protection for your dependents, but that you may thereby reap financial advantage yourself. They appeal, not to your sense of responsibility, but to your cupidity. They preach life insurance, not as a boon to the poor and the defenceless, but to the fortunate and the rich. In a word, they have grafted upon the simple life-insurance idea endless investment and gambling schemes, most of which are fallacies and some of which are palpable frauds. Consequently hundreds of thousands profit little, or not at all, from the insurance feature of their contracts. In the majority of cases they ignore it entirely. The real situation was eloquently summed up at the recent New York life-insurance investigation. It then appeared that at least one-third of the insured abandoned their policies, at great loss to themselves, after they had been in force for one or two years. Of those that are left two-thirds, at particular periods, surrender them, taking in exchange certain so-called "cash profits," thus leaving their families unprovided for. In other words, out of every hundred only about twenty have entered the company for the insurance protection; or, if they have, have not yielded to the temptation of a cash reward and abandoned it.[1]

If we wish mere life insurance unencumbered with

[1] This article was originally published in *McClure's Magazine* for May, 1906. At that time the conditions prevailed which it described. On January 1, 1907, however, the laws passed by the New York Legislature as a result of the Armstrong insurance investigation became effective. These laws prohibit deferred dividends and require all companies to issue certain standard policies of a non-investment and non-gambling character. Unless the new laws are repealed, the New York companies will therefore deal hereafter in straight legitimate life insurance. At present nearly all their outstanding insurance is of the kind described in the present article, which in itself is sufficient reason for permitting it to stand as written.

modern improvements we must go to Connecticut, Massachusetts, New Jersey, and one or two other states. There we shall find great companies limiting their activities to one single end—the insuring of lives. They do not deal in investments, do not act as savings banks or lotteries. They collect from the insured during life certain stipulated sums, and, in the event of death, pay over to the widows certain equivalent indemnities. They collect from each member precisely the same pro rata price for the particular service rendered, and base this price upon certain well-known mathematical laws which closely determine the exact cost. They treat all the insured upon a strictly " mutual basis," which, in the last analysis, means insurance at its actual cost, and that actual cost to all. They furnish this article at a lower price than present quotations for the New York variety. They do it, too, without the elaborate machinery found so indispensable upon Manhattan Island. They have no subsidiary banks or trust companies; no string of office buildings stretched all over the civilised world; no alliance with captains of industry in Wall Street; no array of extravagantly salaried officers; no corruptionists in every important state capitol. They do not have enormous surpluses unjustly withheld from the policy-holders to whom they belong; do not pay in commissions for new business larger sums than that business is worth; do not write insurance in forty-five states and all foreign countries, including China, Japan, Borneo, and Malaysia; they remain quietly at home insuring only respectable heads of American families in good physical condition.

NO REAL DIVIDENDS IN LIFE INSURANCE

Before this story is told in detail, we must have a clear conception of what life insurance, stripped of its mystifications and falsehoods, actually is. We must acquaint ourselves with the ordinary terms of the business: the premium, the reserve, the surplus. Upon no other subject is the public ignorance so profound. And yet, in itself, hardly any subject is more simple. Necessarily, first we must disabuse our minds of certain preconceptions. Life insurance, for example, is not a business. It is not an enterprise in which capital engages for the sake of profit. There are stock companies, but for the most part they pretend that they provide life insurance at its actual cost; that all so-called "profits" go to the insured. Theoretically, at least, and in many instances actually, these great companies are trusts, in the real meaning of the term; their directors are trustees in the most sacred sense. Similarly, life insurance is not gambling. As now practised, certain lottery attachments have been added to it; at times it has been reduced almost to the par of faro and roulette. Above all, life insurance is not an investment. The word " dividend " applied to it has been the most prolific cause of evil. Properly, as will be explained soon, there is no such thing. There can be no dividend, no profit—no investment—because, even under the most favourable circumstances, the expenses of management are so great. For every dollar collected by a life-insurance company it expends anywhere from eighteen to fifty cents in expenses; manifestly it cannot invest the rest so as to pay you any investment return.

LIFE INSURANCE MERELY INDEMNITY—NOT INVESTMENT

Life insurance is one thing, and one thing only. In the social and economic order it performs a single and a simple service. It is the money indemnification for the destruction of a valuable human life. We insure our lives for the same reason that we insure our houses and our ships. All three things have money value; all stand momentarily in danger of destruction; and all are insured for the purpose of recouping ourselves and our dependents for their loss. This protection is something that we buy. We pay money for it; that is, it is an outgo—an expenditure; never an income. Our compensation is the great one that, when we die, our dependents will not be beggared. This is so great an advantage, it adds so wonderfully to the sum of human happiness, that we are willing to pay for it all that it costs. No one regards the insurance upon his house—one's fire insurance—as an investment—as something upon which he receives an annual income; and no more should he so regard the insurance upon his life.

With certain limitations, which will be detailed subsequently, life insurance is a science. It is scientific because it deals with one of the few certainties of human experience—that is, death itself. If a company contracts to pay a certain amount at death it knows that it will have to fulfil that promise; it knows, that is, that the insured will die. Furthermore, it knows, within certain limits, when he will die. It cannot predict this in the individual case, of course. It does not know when *you* will die or when *I* will die; but, if it insures a sufficient number of persons of your age, it knows how many of them will die each year. A mysterious law apparently regulates their taking off. It might have, for example, 100,000 men aged 30, living in London; another 100,000 aged 30, living in New York; another 100,000 aged 30, living in San Francisco. At the end of the first year it will find that 840 out of its London group have died; 840 out of its New York group; 840 out of its San Francisco group. At the end of the

second year 844 will have quietly dropped out of each
of the three groups. In the tenth year 885 in each
group will die; and so on, the original 100,000 being
regularly and gradually diminished every twelvemonth.
In the sixty-sixth year only three or four men in each
of the three groups will be alive; and these, at the ripe
age of 96, will pay their final tribute to nature. There
may, of course, be slight variations in this programme;
but these will not be sufficiently marked to disturb any
calculations based upon them. For all practical purposes the uniformity is so pronounced as to merit the
name of a natural law. This law has been the gradual
discovery of the last two centuries. It has been found
out purely by observation. The records of many English
parishes, the births for particular years, and the records of the deaths through succeeding years, have been
carefully tabulated. Census returns of particular towns
and counties have been compared with the death returns.
Above all, the experience of the life-insurance companies themselves has been taken as a guide.

Before this mortality law was discovered, life insurance was the favourite device for swindling rogues. It
was unsafe; invariably failed; and was consequently
held in the utmost disrepute. Since this law was discovered and honestly utilised life insurance has been a
science. Any merchant who knew just what his expend-

itures would be through a long series of years, and who had the power to adjust his income so as to equal them, could not possibly fail. That is the position of the life-insurance company. Any accurate mortality table, common honesty, and good executive judgment—with these as capital no life-insurance company could possibly collapse. Fire, marine, and other forms of insurance are not thus scientifically based. These companies cannot figure in advance their future losses. No natural laws regulate the burning of houses or the destruction of ships.

TWO SCIENTIFIC BASES OF LIFE INSURANCE—MORTALITY LAW AND INTEREST RATE

The application of this mortality law to the cost of life insurance may now be illustrated in its simplest form. Let us take 1000 men, all aged 40, who desire to insure their lives. They might take out policies in some existing company, but not necessarily—they can carry their insurance just as well themselves. So they enrol themselves into what may be called a life-insurance association. They agree that $1000 shall be paid to the widows of all that die. The association also decides to start with a fund precisely large enough to pay all policy claims as they mature. All members will pay into this fund their pro rata share in advance. In other words, the association decides to adopt what is known as the *single premium* system. Its only problem is the practical determination of what this single payment should be. Obviously, since there are 1000 members and $1000 is to be paid on the death of each, the association will have to pay out ultimately $1,000,000. By the aid of its mortality tables it calculates in advance the payments to be made each year. It finds, according to these tables, that the limit of human life is ninety-six years; inasmuch as all members are in their fortieth year, its payments will range along a series of fifty-six years.[2] In the earlier years these deaths will be comparatively few, and few payments will therefore have to be made. In twenty or thirty years, as the members become older, deaths, and consequently death payments, will become more numerous. In forty years both will decrease—simply because there will be fewer members left to die. In the fifty-sixth year the ultimate survivor, ninety-six years old, will die, and the association will pay out its last $1000 to his heirs.

In all, therefore, the association will pay its $1,000,-

[2] Actually, according to the American experience table, not one out of 1000 starting at age forty would be alive at age ninety-six. If we wish perfect accuracy we should have to base our illustration upon 78,106 lives, the number living at forty of 100,000 starting at age ten. Of this 78,106, the last three will die at age ninety-six. The above illustrations are based upon 1000 lives, however, for the sake of complete clearness.

000 out in fifty-six annual sums. To meet these obligations it will not need to have in hand, at the beginning, a sum of $1,000,000. If all members should die the day immediately following its organisation, $1,000,000 would actually be required. But the deaths will be distributed annually through half a century. If the association started with $1,000,000, it would be guilty of rank extravagance, because money, properly invested, earns interest. The association would need, therefore, not $1,000,000, but a sum which, properly invested, would produce that amount precisely in the annual instalments required. Before deciding what contributions to levy upon its members, the association would have to decide upon the rate at which to invest its funds. If it assumes a high rate, it would not need so large a cash fund; if a small rate, it would need much more. In case of a high rate, that is, its interest earnings would contribute more to the annual sums required than in case its interest rates were low. But the association must exercise much conservatism. Its contracts extend through half a century. That is a long time; and the interest rate fluctuates. If the association should adopt a high rate, it might, after a few years, find itself unable to earn it. Therefore it would not realise the annual sums required to meet its death payments; in other words, it would be insolvent. It will therefore

adopt an investment rate so low that it can confidently figure upon earning it through the whole fifty-six years its contracts run. In strict conservatism it may place it as low as three per cent. By the aid of the mortality table, which shows the number of deaths each year, and the adopted interest rate, which shows the amount contributed to the fund by interest earnings, the amount needed by the association, when it starts, can be mathematically determined. The first year, for example, the association must pay out $9000 to the widows of the nine members who die. To meet that payment the association must have, not $9000, but a sum which, invested at 3 per cent. for one year, will equal $9000. Such a sum is approximately $8730. In the second year the association must pay out $9000 to the widows of nine more deceased members. It must thus have in hand, at the start, a sum which, compounded at 3 per cent. interest for two years, will aggregate $9000. That is, it will need only $8460. The amount needed to have in hand, at the beginning, to meet each year's payments, it thus fully calculates in advance. By adding these fifty-six separate results it has the total cash fund required. By dividing this result by 1000, the original number of the association, it has each member's precise contribution to the fund.

At the beginning, therefore, it is plain why life insurance, in the usual commercial sense, is not an investment. The company puts your premiums at interest, not that it may furnish you a return in addition to the insurance, but that it may accumulate a fund out of which the policy itself is paid.

In its bare essentials this is all there is to life insurance. This great institution rests upon two solid bases: the law of human mortality and that of compound interest. Theoretically only one is indispensable: the mortality law. This enables the company to foresee, for a long period of years, its annual expenditures, and consequently to make provision for their payment. With this principle alone, however, life insurance would not be an accomplished reality, because its cost would be excessive. The interest element, by making life insurance cheap, brings it within the purview of the poorest citizen. It transforms life insurance from an unutilised theory into a most salutary fact. In dealing in both these principles, moreover, we are dealing with moral certainties. Given a certain number of lives of a certain age, nothing is more clearly demonstrated than the order in which they will die. Given a certain amount of money, invested at a certain rate of interest, nothing is more self-evident than its precise accumulation in a given number of years. If all life-insurance companies thus used the same mortality tables—anticipated, in other words, the same number of annual deaths—and invested the premiums at the same rate of interest, the cost of the actual insurance would in all cases be the same.

We have explained this great life-insurance principle on the basis of the *single* premium—the payment down, in a lump sum in advance, of the entire cost of the life insurance—chiefly in the interest of simplicity. As a matter of fact, few buy their life insurance this way. They make to the common fund not one large contribution, but a smaller one each year. A considerable number pay this uniform sum throughout life. They pay, that is, what is technically known as a level premium. The majority pay an annual level premium not through life, but for a stated number of years—twenty, fift·—·, ten, or perhaps five. After this premium-paying period has elapsed, their policy is, in life insurance terms, *paid up*. They pay no more; all they have to do to get the full value is to die. All these various premium systems —annual level, twenty payment, fifteen payment, ten payment, or five—are derived from the single payment, already detailed; all are simply variations of it. All premium calculations are first made upon the theory that the cost is paid in one large sum; and from this result the proper charge, if paid annually through life, or if paid annually for a limited number of years, is deduced. It is hardly worth while to describe in detail how the single premium is thus commuted into these several guises. The explanation involves many details, and the discussion of another subject—that of annuities. It is sufficient to bear in mind that, from the standpoint of the company, the single premium, the annual level premium, the limited payment premiums are all mathematical equivalents.

PAY AS YOU GO SYSTEM A FAILURE

Probably some members of our hypothetical association would propose the method of payment technically known as the *natural* premium. They would divide each year's losses among each year's survivors. If nine men died the first year, necessitating the payment of $9000, they would assess this amount among the 991 who remained. They would tax each man about $9.08. They would likewise assess the next year's losses, another $9000, among the 982 members who survived, making each one's contribution for that year about $9.16. They could make out a plausible argument for this procedure. They would say that this was plain business sense. They would point to the fact that every man paid each year the precise cost of his insurance; and they would assert that this cost would be much lower than under the level premium plan. They would also claim that no large fund would accumulate in the treasury; and that consequently the interest factor could entirely be disregarded. They would clinch their argument by calling attention to the fact that under the level premium plan a thousand dollars' worth of insurance would cost, at its net price, $24 a year; and under the plan they suggest, nine dollars and a few cents the first year, and a slightly increasing price each year thereafter. Indeed, they could make so excellent a case that, had the association not the experience of two centuries to guide it, they would probably carry the day. Theoretically, the natural premium plan is flawless; practically, it never works. It increases the cost of insurance every year; at first almost inappreciably, but later on enormously. In the first year, when the deaths are few—only nine in a thousand—it taxes each member only nine dollars and a few cents. In the thirtieth year, however, the association contains only about 490; that is, 510 have died. That year it loses 29 members and is thus called upon to pay out $29,000; therefore it charges the survivors $62 each. By this time it finds that the increasing annual premium is much larger than the discarded uniform annual premium. But its troubles have only begun. Its members are now all seventy-one years old; and they die very rapidly. The association is thus embarrassed from two standpoints. It has to pay out larger death sums each year, and each year it has fewer members upon whom to assess them. In the case of the last surviving nonagenarian the situation would be absurd. The association—an association now only theoretical because all its members are dead—would have to pay out $1000, but would have no members to levy upon. If it made the natural premiums payable at the beginning of each year the last survivor would have to advance the whole $1000 with which to pay his own death claim.

In this there is nothing actuarially unscientific or unjust. But in practice it never succeeds. It has been tried thousands of times and it is the basis of the numerous assessment and fraternal orders now dying a lingering death. All these associations prosper in the earlier years, when deaths are few and assessments consequently low. All begin to lose members as deaths and assessments increase. Men simply will not pay these largely increased premiums in the later years; consequently they retire and the assessment schemes collapse.

RESERVES: ADVANCE PAYMENTS FOR INSURANCE

The association thus finally decides that each member shall pay for his $1000 insurance by contributing $24 to the common fund each year as long as he lives. It therefore collects in advance from its 1000 members

$24,000 the first year. It promptly invests this at three per cent., thus increasing it in one year to $24,720. It pays out this year only $9000 to the beneficiaries of its nine deceased members. It therefore has left in its treasury $15,720—the amount of all the premiums, plus one year's interest, which has not been used. Dividing this $15,720 fund by 991, the number of surviving members, it has a credit of about $15 to each surviving policy-holder. That is the amount of the first year's premium, plus interest, which has not been used in paying death claims. The association collects $24 the second year from the 991 remaining policy-holders, a total of $23,784. It adds this to the $15,720 in the treasury, thus obtaining a fund of $39,504. It invests this again at three per cent., thus increasing the fund to $40,689. It pays out $9000 as policy claims, thus decreasing the fund to $31,689. It divides this among the 982 remaining members, crediting each with a fund of approximately $32. It finds that that is the amount of each policy-holder's premium for two years, improved at compound interest, which has not been used in paying death claims. It finds, in other words, that it collects from every policy-holder, under the level premium plan, more money than it needs to meet its expenditures, simply because its death losses, in the earlier years, are comparatively few.

The association goes on thirty or forty years; and then develops a new situation. In its thirtieth year it has 490 surviving members. It collects from each $24, and thus from all $11,760, which, with three per cent. interest added, equals $12,112. But it loses by death in the thirtieth year thirty-two and must therefore pay out $32,000. Manifestly this year's income does not suffice for the outgo. It has collected only about $12,000, and must pay out $32,000! The association, therefore, makes up the difference by drawing upon the *unused* payments of the earlier years. By this time its total unused fund—unused premiums, that is, plus compound interest—is very large, and the appropriation for this thirtieth year deficit diminishes it only slightly. The association through the remaining years will never collect enough again to meet its annual payments; every year the deficits will increase; but the accumulations from the unused premiums and interest of the first half of its existence will precisely enable it to come out whole.

The association calls these accumulations on the premium payments of the earlier years its *reserves*. It figures out the accumulation upon each policy, and calls it the *reserve* upon that particular policy. In other words it *reserves* the unused premium payments of the earlier years, when deaths do not devour all the money paid in, and pays them out in the later, when deaths more than use up the annual payments. It must keep these *reserves* simply because it collects its contributions in uniform annual sums, in the earlier years too much, the later years too little, in deference to the majority of its members who insist upon paying that way. In another article the nature of this *reserve* will be analysed in detail. At this point its great importance in life insurance only need be insisted upon. In fact it is the one test of solvency.

If our association honestly reserves these unused early payments it cannot possibly fail. If it steals or wastes them it must ultimately collapse. It could steal them for many years, however, without detection, because for about half its existence it would collect more than enough money each year to pay that year's death losses. When it reached those later years, however, when each year's collections did not pay each year's losses, its dishonesty would stand revealed. Under modern conditions our association would find it difficult to do this. It would find that every state had organised insurance departments to prevent this very thing. Every year all its policies would be inventoried and the amount of necessary reserve on each one computed. If our association did not have that precise amount in its treasury, or assets to cover it—bonds, mortgages, etc.—the receiver would be called in and the shutters go up. Its *reserves*, that is, are an insurance company's *liabilities*. The chief function of the insurance departments is to act as watchdogs of these reserves; and this, whatever their other shortcomings, they successfully do.

One life-insurance association thus discovers the annual price of a $1000 policy at age 40. It has thus determined, however, merely the *net* cost; the cost, that is, of the actual insurance. It has made no provision for the second element of cost in life insurance; that is, the expenses of company management. But it must have a chief manager of the fund—a president, several assistants, clerks, and office boys. It must have an office in which to conduct business; furniture, stationery, postage, and so on. Above all, unless all its 1000 members join spontaneously, it must have a lively force of insinuating gentlemen to persuade them in—that is, life-insurance agents. All these things, especially the agency force, cost money. For want of a better system the association clumsily adds to every premium a certain annual sum to provide a special fund to meet these expenses. Perhaps it increases the annual premiums from $24 to $32—the extra $8 being for expenses. It calls this addition a *loading*. Its total premium, in other

words, consists of two parts: the amount actually needed
to meet all death claims, as indicated by a mortality
table, and decreased by interest earnings at a particular rate; and the amount added to cover the cost of
management.

WHY THERE IS A SURPLUS: THREE SOURCES OF GAIN

When the company applies these hypothetical rates
to the actual business of insuring lives, however, the
situation changes. It finds that the scheme does not
work with quite the precision anticipated. It discovers
that the deaths do not occur quite as the mortality
table provides; that the interest rate earned is not
always three per cent.; that the expenses do not always
amount to the same sum as the loadings. It finds that
it has based its charges upon three separate theories—
a theory concerning the yearly death-rate, a theory
concerning the interest earned, and a theory concerning the expense of management. Its theory concerning the death-rate pretty closely coincides with the
facts; its theory concerning the interest rate shows
greater divergence; and its theory concerning the management expenses is usually woefully mistaken. If its
death-rate were precisely that indicated by the tables;
if it earned precisely the three per cent. interest figured
upon, not a penny more, not a penny less; if it spent

in management expenses precisely the amounts provided in the premium loadings; the cost of insurance
would manifestly be precisely what was charged. Because all these factors vary, and vary, too, from year
to year, the actual cost of insurance varies, also from
year to year. But, fortunately for the cause of life
insurance, it varies always in one direction. The company's charges, that is, always exceed the actual cost.
It almost invariably has *fewer* death losses than the
mortality tables indicate; and it commonly earns *more*
interest than the estimate assumes. That is to say, it
pays out each year less than it has provided for; and
earns, in interest, *more* than it needs to pay all claims.
A company properly conducted also uses less every
year for expenses than the amount provided in the
premium loadings.

FIRST POSSIBLE SAVING: FROM MORTALITY

These several gains depend, of course, upon the
honesty and ability with which the company is managed. Its mortality table is that formulated by Sheppard Homans in 1865 from the actual experience of
The Mutual Life. That table is based upon selected
lives—lives that have been insured, and consequently
assumed to have been in at least average good health.
If the company's medical department is inefficient or

corrupt, if it insures consumptives, paralytics, and physical degenerates, either because it knows no better or is impelled by the furious ambition of the management to do a large business, manifestly its mortality showing will be bad, perhaps even sinking below the standard of the table. But if it exercises unusual care, and takes people only in the finest physical condition, it will make a much better showing than the table; the company will not have to pay as much in death losses as it supposed; therefore it will have a considerable " saving from mortality."

SECOND POSSIBLE SAVING: FROM INTEREST

If it invests the premiums with bad judgment or dishonestly; if it buys depreciated bonds merely because its investment department has been annexed by a Wall Street banking house; if its directors constantly unload upon it, at a good profit to themselves, investments which they themselves have purchased on the quiet; if its directors receive a substantial " rake off " on every investment made, evidently it will make a bad showing on its interest earnings. But if it invests the premiums with good judgment, it will make more than the interest rate required. Its premium prices, for example, may be based upon a three per cent. investment rate; three per cent., that is, is all it must earn to pay obligations.

But by carefully making investments it may actually earn four or five or even six. That is, it earns one, two, or three per cent. more than it needs. It thus has a " saving from interest."

THIRD POSSIBLE SAVING: FROM MANAGEMENT EXPENSES

Again, if the company is extravagantly conducted; if it has many and ridiculously salaried officers; if it pays out enormous sums in commissions to agents, and supplies them, gratis, with travelling bags and fountain pens—manifestly it will swallow all, frequently more, than its " loadings." But if the machine is economically managed, it will save a considerable portion of the expense charges. There will thus be a " saving from loadings."

Every company, as has been said, shows these savings every year, though in varying degrees. Every company, that is, charges the policy-holder more than the insurance actually costs. It is not properly subject to criticism for this. It cannot foresee, in advance, precisely what that charge should be. It bases its prices upon a mortality table which, for all practical purposes, is correct; upon an interest rate so low that it can certainly be earned; upon an expense rate which, even under the most adverse circumstances, should be sufficient. It charges this excess so as to be absolutely on the safe side—so that it may surely meet all its obligations.

Thus, inevitably, at the end of each year, the company has in its treasury a goodly sum, representing money taken from the policy-holders in excess of the real cost of the insurance. This is popularly known as its *surplus*. The surplus thus measures the difference between the theoretical and the actual cost. It is the precise amount which the policy-holders have been overcharged. "What," say the directors, "ought we to do with it? We have paid all our policy obligations and laid by for reserve the precise amount needed for our future payments, and have this extra amount on our hands which we do not need and can never legitimately use. We do not need to keep it until next year, because there will also be a surplus left over after next year's business. Must we spend this surplus in some foolish way? Give it to charity? Put it in our own pockets?" The puzzle is easily solved. What, according to its professions, does the company exist for? Simply to furnish life insurance to its members at its exact, mathematically ascertained cost. It finds, at the end of each year, that it has charged too much. Obviously it should return to the policy-holders the amount of that overcharge.

These repayments of "surplus" are what are popularly called "dividends." They are the "profits" of life insurance. They are the "investment return" on your premium. Actually they are none of these things. They are simply the repayment of the excess cost of the insurance. Let us seek a homely comparison. You send a messenger-boy to buy you a quantity of cigars. Not being sure what the exact cost will be you give him a two-dollar bill. He pays $1.50 and returns with you cigars and fifty cents change. You would hardly regard that fifty cents as a "dividend" upon your purchase of cigars. Your messenger-boy has simply returned your overpayment. Your position is precisely the same when you buy a policy of life insurance. Your company does not know, at the beginning of the year, what the exact cost will be, but, to be on the safe side, charges you an excess price. At the end of the year it gives you back—or at least it should—your change, and miscalls it a "dividend." If agreeable, instead of actually taking the fifty cents change from the messenger-boy, you might send him back to buy more cigars with it. Similarly, instead of taking your life-insurance "dividend" in cash, you might let the insurance company keep it and give you the extra amount of insurance it will buy. Again, you might let the messenger-boy keep the fifty cents because you intend to send him to buy cigars a few days hence. Similarly, you might let the insurance company keep the " dividend," and apply it to buy your insurance next year; that is, to reduce the next year's premium.

Many of our largest insurance companies differ from this messenger-boy in one important respect. He usually comes back with your fifty cents. Most insurance companies, however, in the case of a majority of their policy-holders, do not come promptly back with the annual overpayments. They hold the change.

When the people complain that the current price of life insurance is excessive, they simply mean that these overpayments are not returned—or at least not in the proportion that they are paid in. If the companies are honestly and ably managed and these overpayments are. equitably returned, there could not possibly be any excess cost. Thus we have formulated a rule by which we can measure the relative prices charged by the several companies. If we take the actual premium paid each year and subtract from this each year's " dividends," or returned overpayments, we shall have the actual net prices charged for the insurance.

INSURANCE COST WHEN THESE OVERCHARGES ARE
ANNUALLY RETURNED

Let this rule therefore be applied to several companies, all of unquestioned solvency. You are forty
years old, in good health, and seek a $10,000 ordinary
policy of life insurance. You decide first, for example,
upon the Connecticut Mutual. You are charged an
annual premium of $309.40. After a year the com-
pany finds that it has overcharged you precisely
$38.50,[1] and returns that in the guise of a " dividend."
Manifestly your insurance has cost you exactly
$270.90. You pay $309.40 the second year. After
this has passed, the Connecticut Mutual finds it has
overcharged you $41.50, and sends you a check for
that sum. This year your insurance has cost $267.90—
a little less than the year before. You pay regularly
for several years the same $309.40; and every year the
amount paid back at its end increases. In the twentieth
year you pay the same $309.40; but at its end receive
back a check for $91.50 [1]—thus decreasing the net in-
surance cost to $217.90.

Thus each year you receive a larger " dividend ";
each year, that is, the actual cost of your insurance is
decreased. The explanation is, briefly, that the *reserve*

[1] According to 1906 scale of dividends.

on your policy, as is explained above, grows larger every year, and the interest earned on it each year therefore increases. Suppose that at the same time you took your $10,000 policy in the Connecticut Mutual, you had taken an identical policy in the Mutual Benefit. You would pay the same initial premium, $309.40. In this case, instead of taking your " dividend " in cash, you might advantageously buy additional insurance with it. Your " dividend," that is, would be regarded as a single premium, and the amount purchased placed to the credit of the policy. At the end of the first year, therefore, instead of $10,000 insurance, you would have in the neighbourhood of $10,158. As in the Connecticut Mutual, your " dividends " would increase every year. In twenty years, if you used them to buy this additional insurance, your policy, originally for $10,000, would have increased to one for about $13,000. If you had taken out similar policies in the Northwestern Mutual of Milwaukee, the State Mutual of Massachusetts, the Massachusetts Mutual, and a few other so-called annual dividend companies, the results would have been similarly favourable. Your policy would constantly grow larger or its actual annual cost would steadily decrease. Both results would be explained by the fact that the companies, at the end of each year, returned to you the overcharge made at the beginning.

INSURANCE COST WHEN THIS OVERCHARGE IS "DE-FERRED" OR "ACCUMULATED"

Let us suppose, however, that, at the same time that you entered the Connecticut Mutual and the other annual-dividend or annual-repayment companies, you took a $10,000 policy in the Equitable. You pay $330.10—more than $20 more at the beginning than the other companies charge. You hold the policy a year, but receive back from the company not a single penny of your overcharge! Thus far you have paid $330.10 in the Equitable for precisely the same policy that cost you $270.90 in the Connecticut Mutual—a difference of $59.20. The Equitable charges you $20 more in the first place, and then neglects to pay back the excess price. Perhaps, at the same time, you take out another $10,000 policy in the New York Life. You pay precisely the same initial price that you paid the Equitable—that is, $330.10. A year passes; you get back no overcharge. You have also taken a $10,000 in the Mutual Life. You pay $327.60—slightly less than in the Equitable and New York Life; and also fail to get back your overpayment. All your excess payments—all your "dividends," if you wish—are tightly locked up in the company's vault.

You note that this procedure differs from that of

the "smaller companies," and you write for an explanation. The Equitable informs you that you have a " deferred dividend " policy; the Mutual that you have a
" distribution " policy; the New York Life that you
have an " accumulation " policy. You inquire the
meaning of these somewhat doubtful expressions; and
learn that in the Equitable your " dividends " are not
paid annually, but " deferred " for a certain period,
usually twenty years; that in the Mutual they are held,
also usually for twenty years and then " distributed ";
and that in the New York Life they are " accumulated " for twenty years and then paid back. By in-
quiring more deeply, however, you learn that these
Equitable " dividends " are not necessarily " deferred "
for your benefit, but, in the majority of cases, for the
benefit of others; that the Mutual's, after being held
for twenty years, will not necessarily be " distributed "
to *you,* but, it is more than likely, to some one else;
that those of the New York Life, after being " accumulated " for twenty years, are quite likely to be paid
over to Tom, Dick, or Harry. You learn that, in two
contingencies, both of which are extremely likely, you
will get no " dividends," no repayments, at all. If you
should have hard luck, and fail to pay your premiums
for any one of the twenty years the overpayments are
held in the company's treasury, you would forfeit all

these " deferred," " distributed," or " accumulated dividends." If at any time in these twenty years you should
die, you would also forfeit all your overpayments. Only
in case you live for twenty years, and promptly pay
your annual premiums, will you get back your annual
overpayments. And then you get back precisely what
the company sees fit to pay you—not a penny more. If
you study your contract—your policy, that is—you
will learn that the company has not legally obliged
itself to pay you a single dollar! Your share of the
twenty years' accumulated surplus is merely what is
"equitably determined by the actuaries of the company." You find that the company is not obliged to
give you any accounting; to tell you how much has been
" saved " from your premiums each year; to let you
know whether they have been carefully kept, or whether
they have been squandered. If you could get at the
company's books, you would learn that, in fact, it keeps
no actual account; that it lumps all its annual overpayments or " dividends " in one sum, and not until
the nineteenth year makes any attempt to determine
how much should come to *you* and how much to *me*. If,
angered by these discoveries, you attempted to haul the
Equitable, the Mutual, and the New York Life to court
and demand, as a policy-holder, to learn precisely what
your dividend amounts to, you would find that there is

a law that, in effect, prevents you from doing this very thing. In other words, in taking a deferred dividend policy you had authorised the company to keep your accumulated overpayments for twenty years; to pay them back to you only in the event that you had not died or lapsed; to pay back then only such small sums as it might choose; and to render you no accounting whatever and to keep none!

POOR DISCRIMINATED AGAINST IN FAVOUR OF RICH

This elaborate machinery, you will discover, has been admittedly evolved for the purpose of perpetrating a great injustice. The company declines to pay back these excess charges to those who die or drop their policies in order that it may pay them, instead, to those who live and persist. In other words, it does not treat all its insured upon an equal basis; does not charge all the same price for their insurance; does not preserve "mutuality." It discriminates, too, against its least fortunate members. Manifestly, if you die, your widow needs these dividends, or the insurance they represent, much more than if you live. The deferred dividend companies take this money from the widows of their dead members and give it to their persisting policy-holders. Again, if you lapse your policy, it is usually because you haven't the money to continue it. The deferred div-

idend companies take advantage of this misfortune to
deprive you of certain equities. Your " dividends " go
to swell the account of those who have been able to
keep up their regular payments. The deferred dividend
plan is thus clearly a discrimination against the unfortunate in favour of the prosperous. It overcharges most
—and they the less prosperous—in order that it may
undercharge a few—and they the more fortunate.
Actually, as we shall see, it does not even treat its
minority fairly. Far from paying back to the persistent the " dividends " of all who die and lapse, it does
not always pay back their own!

Let us imagine, for a moment, a savings bank organised on this basis. It requires all depositors to leave
with it stipulated sums each year. It declines to pay
interest annually, but proposes to hold all earnings in
its own treasury for twenty years. It is not obliged to
keep an accounting of the earnings; in fact does keep
no accounting; and has secured the passage of a state
law that prevents any depositor from demanding one.
It will pay these accumulated earnings only after twenty
years, and then pays just what its trustees deem fair
and " equitable." To depositors who have died in that
twenty years it will pay no interest at all; when they
die their widows get simply the principal. To those who
fail to keep up their annual deposits they will pay no

interest. If they drop out, they get simply the original sums paid in. After twenty years, however, the trustees promise to pay to all who live and have regularly made deposits, all the earnings accumulated upon the deposits of those who have died or " lapsed." In the end, however, many of the favoured few will discover that they have not only not received these additional sums, but not always the entire interest upon their own deposits.

That is the gist of the much-discussed " deferred dividend " policy. As will be explained, this is only the survival of a scheme which was much worse. This is what the great Henry B. Hyde called " semi-tontine "—half tontine. His pet plan, whole " Tontine," was so iniquitous that it was virtually suppressed by law.

Let us see how the idea practically works itself out. Every insurant on the deferred dividend plan belongs to one of three classes: he pays his premium for a few years and then lapses; he pays and dies; he pays and survives the deferred dividend period. Let us suppose that he belongs to the first class. He has a $10,000 policy in the Equitable, for which he pays $330 a year. He pays for fifteen years; then is forced by adverse circumstances or other reasons to drop his policy. He gets back $2784. This is his so-called surrender more they would have received dividends amounting to $17,000. Had he taken an annual policy, purchased each year additional insurance with his dividends, his family would have received about $77,000 when he died. All these advantages he lost merely by dying six days before his policy matured. On a smaller scale that episode is repeated hundreds of times every day.

SIXTY PER CENT. GET NO DIVIDENDS AT ALL

According to the actual experience of the three big New York companies, sixty per cent. of all their deferred dividend policy-holders either die or lapse before the termination of the deferred dividend period. In other words, sixty per cent. of all their policy-holders do not get back the sums they are annually overcharged for their insurance. Sixty per cent. have absolutely no chance of getting out whole. If these sixty per cent. should take policies in the companies which annually returned their surplus, they could peacefully die without depriving their families of the protection actually paid for in good cash; or retire from the companies without losing the large amounts they had unnecessarily paid in.

Evidently the remaining forty per cent. constitute the fortunate class who *live and pay.* As a reward they are to receive not only their own overpayments, but

the overpayments of all the unfortunate who have died
and the poverty-stricken who have lapsed. Forty per
cent. of the policy-holders, that is, are to get, not
only their own "dividends," but the "dividends" of
the sixty per cent. who get none. Their deferred dividends, swelled from these two sources, evidently should
be enormous. They were persuaded to leave their overpayments for ten, fifteen, or twenty years—usually
twenty—by certain "estimates" as to profits, officially
issued by the companies. They did not insure primarily to protect their families, but to get the large sums
of which so many hundreds of thousands of unfortu-
nates have been deprived. They have played the game
and have won. What have been the gains? Let us see
first what they were led to expect, and how these
expectations were fulfilled. In 1873, for example, you
took out a $10,000 policy in the Equitable. What you
got was not then described as a "deferred dividend,"
but a "Tontine-Savings Fund policy." You paid a
premium of $313 for twenty years—a total of $6260.
Your agent informed you that by leaving your "dividends"—your overpayments, that is—with the company you would get, at the end of the twenty-year
period, a cash bonus of $9556 in addition to the in-
surance. Your "investment return"—your "savings
fund"—plus the life insurance, would amount to that

much. Your friends who insured in 1874, 1875, 1876, 1877, and 1878 were furnished the same estimate of winnings. You paid your premiums faithfully for twenty years, and grew grey-haired so doing, constantly having ahead the large sum which was to lighten the cares of old age. In 1893, instead of getting a check for $9556, you got one for $4365—a drop of 55 per cent. You paid $6260 exclusive of interest; had expected an investment return of $3296 and had realised an investment deficit of $1895—a total disappointment of $5190. However, you were among the lucky ones. Your friend who had insured in 1874 in the expectation of getting $9556, got in 1894 only $4105; your friend who insured in 1875, under the same hallucination, got in 1895 only $3795. The "dividend" dropped in 1897 to $3415, in 1901 to $3110, in 1904 to $2850! You had not earned these "dividends" yourself; they were not your "overpayments"; they were your overpayments plus your share of the overpayments of thousands of dead and unfortunate men who had been grossly overcharged all these years.

DEFERRED DIVIDENDS FREQUENTLY EXCEEDED
BY ANNUAL

All this time the old-fashioned companies have paid their " dividends " annually; have paid back to each policy-holder each year precisely his own overpayments. They have not paid *me* the surplus that belongs to *you;* nor to *you* the surplus that belongs to *me;* they have treated us all fairly and honestly, and given us all our insurance at its actual cost. In spite of this in many cases they have paid annual dividends to all who have insured actually more than the New York companies have paid to forty per cent. The New York companies arrange their policy-holders chiefly in three classes: those who wait ten, fifteen, and twenty years for their " dividends." Ten years' annual " dividends " in the old-fashioned companies regularly amount to more than the ten-year " dividend " in the New York companies. In fact, the showing is so much against the latter companies that they no longer publish their results. The same is true of the fifteen-year periods. If you took a $10,000 policy at forty—or almost any other age—in the Connecticut Mutual in 1890—your insurance cost—the premiums for fifteen years, less the cash value at the end of fifteen years— would amount to $776.50. In the Equitable for the same period, and on the same basis of comparison, your insurance would have cost $951.70. In spite of the fact that you ran no risk of losing your "dividends" by death or lapse in the Connecticut company, your insurance actually cost you $175.20 less than in the New York concern, in which you daily ran such risk. If we extend the comparison to the twenty-year classes, here also occasionally, though not uniformly, the New York companies make an unfavourable showing.

Normally, of course, annual "dividends" could hardly be expected to compare favourably with deferred; because, as already explained, the latter are swelled by the forfeited "dividends" of the sixty per cent. who do not survive the deferred dividend periods. In justice to the annual companies we should compare their "dividends" with the annual "dividends" paid in New York. The Equitable, the Mutual, and the New York Life, if forced to it, will issue annual policies. They pay higher commissions on the other kind; but still they carry a considerable amount of insurance on the annual plan. Only by comparing results on these identical policies does the extravagance of the larger companies stand revealed. The "dividends" paid by the outside companies, on identically the same policies, are frequently nearly twice the amounts paid in New York.

In a word, the biggest New York companies enormously overcharge the insured. The surpluses of which they boast so largely in part measure the extent of this overcharge. These surpluses, of course, are not properly surpluses at all. The Equitable, in its report for 1905, claims a surplus of nearly $81,000,000.[5] Of that, $71,000,000 consists of withheld " dividends." The Equitable retains this vast sum by virtue of the deferred dividend scheme; it is money, which, according to its own claim, it keeps in its treasury instead of distributing among those to whom it belongs—the policy-holders. It calls this surplus " strength "; more properly we should call it " injustice." The Mutual has some $70,000,000 similarly withheld; the New York Life some $47,000,000. These companies have these great surpluses simply because they do not promptly return the excess cost of insurance; the outside companies have proportionately small surpluses because they do. When the Equitable advertises that it has a surplus of $80,000,000 it brazenly makes public its policy of overcharging its insured. The New York

[5] This was afterwards cut down by the Superintendent of Insurance to $67,000,000.

Life, in boasting of its $47,000,000, the Mutual, in boasting of its $70,000,000, lay themselves open to the same charge. An insurance company with a big surplus occupies precisely the same position as a government with a big surplus. In both cases the surplus means the same thing. In a government it means that the people have been overtaxed; in a life-insurance company it means that they have been overcharged.

One great difference there is, however. A great government is responsible for every penny of its surplus. A life-insurance company is not. Its policy contracts are so written, as has been explained, that it can turn over to the insured just as much, or just as little, as it pleases. The Equitable can pay back to its policy-holders the whole $71,000,000 deferred dividend surplus, or not a penny. Mr. Ryan, who owns a majority of the stock of the Equitable, could dump anywhere from $50,000,000 to $60,000,000 into the sewer and still be entirely able to meet all his policy obligations. In addition to this surplus, be it remembered, the Equitable has nearly $450,000,000 in reserves; that is the amount it must keep on hand in order to be solvent. All above that figure is surplus—unnecessary amounts collected from policy-holders. Its managers can use the whole amount in wasteful expenditure; and yet, according to court decisions, no one can hold them

to account. Moreover, they can spend the whole amount
and yet not endanger the company's solvency!

And thus the story of life insurance in this country
is the story of the surplus. It is this accumulation of
the excess cost of the insurance which has debauched
the life-insurance companies. Mr. Hyde, Mr. McCurdy,
and Mr. McCall have had constantly at their disposal
these enormous sums. They have been able to defer
their repayment for twenty years; and have then been
obliged to pay back only such small sums as they chose.
Instead of paying it back, they have dissipated enormous sums. Did they wish to increase their salaries?
There was the surplus from which such increases could
be taken. Did they wish to make provision for a large
number of poor relations? They promptly set them all
to feeding upon the surplus. Does Henry B. Hyde
need some $600,000 to save one of his demoralised
banks from insolvency? The Equitable's surplus provides the necessary amount. Do they all control certain
trust companies which require large deposits with which
the stock market may be played and big dividends
earned? The surplus furnishes anywhere from $10,-
000,000 to $30,000,000 for this benevolent purpose.

Does Mr. Hyde need money to rent space and furnish up safe deposit vaults for a com; iny controlled by himself and friends? Why, take it out f the surplus, of course! Is Mr. McCall moved to contr ute $150,000 to several Republican campaign funds? Again the surplus is drawn upon. Is a fund of som $1,300,000 needed for the purpose of bribing legislatoi s? The surplus will not mind a little thing like that. Are $3,000,000 or $4,000,-000 needed to help float certain unfloatable bonds? Again there is the surplus. Above all, do the companies require large sums to pay extravagant commissions to a corrupt agency force, so that they may bring in more policy-holders who will begin piling up more surplus? Does the New York Life need $13,000,000 for this purpose above the charges for commissions actually provided in this same new business? It is quietly " borrowed " from the surplus. And so on. The companies have no desire, however extravagant and expensive, which the long-suffering surplus cannot gratify. The surplus maintains Houses of Mirth at Albany; dines the French Ambassador; conveys young Mr. Hyde and his friends all over the United States in private palace-cars; supports an endless array of bygone political hacks; pensions " rantankerous friends from up the river," and other custodians of dangerous life-insurance secrets; provides United States Senators with $20,000 yearly retainers; keeps in steady employment a fine assortment of journalistic talent ready to sing the praises of New York life insurance. The policy-holders slave year after year building that surplus up; the methods of Mr. Hyde, Mr. McCall, and Mr. McCurdy have contributed quite as much toward pulling it down. The actual sum standing on each company's books is the resultant of these two opposing forces.

In the last analysis, then, what is the surplus? It is what is left of the policy-holders' overpayments for " dividend " purposes, after certain extravagant and reckless managements have finished dipping into them. In fact, as will be shown subsequently, the present surplus system was created for this very purpose. Henry Baldwin Hyde, the man who devised the plan, did so largely that he might quietly make money out of his great trust. How Mr. Hyde, by aid of his surplus, demoralised the whole life insurance business, and induced the present scandals—this is the story which will be told in subsequent chapters.

CHAPTER II

THE PIONEER

AMERICAN life insurance really had its beginning at an English breakfast table. John Kenyon, the well-known poet and entertainer, was the host. Robert Browning, Samuel Rogers, Elizabeth Barrett, Miss Mittford, and Barry Cornwall were among the more notable guests. Less conspicuous was a dark-eyed, dark-haired American who had arrived only a few days before from Boston in the somewhat humble guise of a book agent, but whose previous labours for liberty and philanthropy, to say nothing of his fine bearing and brilliant wit, were a sufficient passport into the most distinguished circles.

Barry Cornwall and Elizur Wright, the American book agent, sat side by side and soon found many topics in common. Wright gave entertainingly his impressions of London, and described with enthusiasm his recent visit to the Sun Life-Insurance office and his talk with Joshua Milne, the author of the Carlisle table of mortality. His trip to London, Wright explained, was partly to investigate English life-insurance conditions in the interest of the Massachusetts companies, and he had already learned a great deal about the subject that was new to him.

" Life Insurance! " interrupted Cornwall. " Why, it's the greatest humbug in Christendom! "

ENGLISH POLICY-HOLDERS SOLD OUT AT THE ROYAL EXCHANGE

To prove his statement Cornwall invited Wright to visit the Royal Exchange the succeeding Thursday afternoon. They found in progress an auction upon life-insurance policies. The bidders were chiefly Hebrew speculators. The victims, for the most part, were old men who had put practically all their savings into their life insurance, and who now found themselves unable to continue their payments. They could get nothing back from the companies for what they had paid in. The great modern principle of surrender values was as yet unrecognised. The insured, in the event of lapse, were thus compelled to dispose of their policies to sharpers for such cash sums as they would bring. The purchasers, of course, by continuing the payments, received the face of the policies at death. They gambled, that is, upon the chance that their victims would die early. Wright was informed that these auctions took place every Thursday afternoon. He saw them regularly advertised in the newspapers. He found

that a considerable part of the speculative public made
fortunes in this way, and he discovered one venturesome
individual who had thus picked up forty-two policies.
He was also told that the custom frequently incited to
crime.

Wright declared that he had attended many slave
auctions at home, but that they seemed little worse to
him than this British custom. He learned, however, that
it was only typical of the general injustice on which the
whole British life-insurance system rested. His London
visit took place in 1844, and the business by that time
had largely fallen into the hands of swindlers. The
chancery courts were constantly clogged with defunct
companies. In twenty-five years nearly three hundred
offices had been chartered; in the same period nearly
two hundred and fifty had failed. Amalgamations, em-
bezzlements, reinsurances—these were the order of the
day. A few years after Wright's visit, seventy-eight
life-insurance schemes scandalously wound up. Needy
aristocrats constantly sold their names for this purpose; the favourite device of the bankrupt nobility,
indeed, was the organisation of life companies. They
fitted up elaborate offices, issued high-sounding pros-
pectuses, impressed defunct schoolmasters and clergymen in as canvassers, and for a brief time did
a flourishing business. They paid what were then enor-

mous commissions—thirty-five and forty per cent.; regularly abstracted fifty per cent. of the premiums in " expenses "! and thus soon, in spite of frequently large receipts, found themselves unable to pay their policy claims. At the time of Wright's visit the public conscience was aroused. Dickens had recently satirised the business in " Martin Chuzzlewit," and Parliament had held a futile investigation.

Wright recalled that similar tendencies had manifested themselves at home. They had not reached the same proportions in America, however, probably because the life-insurance business had not yet passed its infant stage. In its undeveloped condition Wright thus saw a great opportunity. He took upon himself a solemn vow. He determined to exert all his powers to save his own country from the humiliation which he had witnessed in England. He had sufficiently studied life insurance to know that it was basicly sound, and that, properly practised, it could be made one of the greatest safeguards of the economic system. For more than forty years, until his death in 1885, Wright devoted his whole life to this end.

EARLY TRAINING AS AN ABOLITIONIST

If any single man was created for the purpose of elevating and preserving life insurance, Elizur Wright

ELIZUR WRIGHT IN 1844

was that man. He united in one personality all the
essential ·intellectual and moral qualities. He had a
great mathematical brain, untiring energy, a keen love
of justice, a strong instinct for battle. He had already
manifested his crusading temper in many unpopular
causes. He was of homespun Connecticut stock, and, a
boy six years old, had been taken by his parents
through " mud, stump, and beechroots " to their new
wilderness home in Ohio. His mental qualities had manifested themselves at an early age; as a child he had
shocked his pious father by pressing arguments against
the Shorter Catechism. At the age of seventeen he
became a student at Yale, earning his education by
ringing the bell, waiting on commons, and tutoring
his classmates. Here his chief relaxations were Web-
ster's conics and Playfair's geometry; and here, too,
his unceasing zeal for certain unfashionable theories
made him unpopular. He preached temperance, and
succeeded in having wines abolished from the Phi Beta
Kappa banquets, and, worse than all, regarded slavery
as the great national sin. Yale College in those days
was full of Southern students, and upon them Wright
frequently exercised his dialectics. His intellectual
capacity, especially in mathematics, so impressed the
teaching force that after graduation he was invited to
return to New Haven as a tutor; but after a year or

two teaching he became Professor of Mathematics at the Western Reserve College, which his father had helped to found. Here, too, his constant and open advocacy of the anti-slavery cause made him detested. He early joined forces with Garrison, wrote frequently in the *Liberator*, and became the close friend and correspondent of Arthur and Lewis Tappan, Beriah Green, and the other early abolitionists. After a few years he abandoned his professorship for anti-slavery journalism and came to New York as editor of the *Anti-Slavery Reporter* and Secretary of the American Anti-Slavery Society. Wright also frequently appeared in the courts in defence of runaway slaves, and was constantly threatened with personal violence. At one time an organised attempt was made by Southerners to kidnap him; a pilot-boat, which was to take him to South Carolina, haunted New York harbour for nearly a month. At another time his house in Brooklyn was threatened by a mob. The Mayor called on Wright and begged him to leave town in order to prevent a riot. Wright refused to budge. " If you can't protect me," he said, " I'll protect myself." Whereupon he placed a huge axe against the door and awaited his foes. Only by stopping the ferries from running was a serious disturbance avoided.

A MAN WITH ALL THE QUALITIES OF A
SUCCESSFUL REFORMER

As it turned out, these were precisely the qualities
needed in his battle with life-insurance dishonesty. The
fight for the policy-holder called for the same sympa-
thies, the same watchful zeal, the same sacrifice of
expediency to conviction as the fight for the slave. In
life insurance, as in the slavery agitation, Wright was
always the radical. To this moral fervour, however, he
added indispensable talents; he had a capacious brain
and marked mathematical genius. In him moral enthusiasm and actuarial science blended. As soon as he
returned from Europe he mingled his anti-slavery
crusade with his struggle for life-insurance reform.
When not calculating life tables he was assisting in
the escape of runaway slaves. He was one of the
" mob " arrested for assisting the flight of the fugitive
Shadrach. In order to preach more effectively his
causes he decided to found a daily newspaper. He
scraped together enough money to buy a quantity of
paper, carried it over to the printer on his own back,
and told that astonished person to begin the first
issue. Thus appeared the *Chronotype*, which many old
Bostonians still remember with intellectual relish.
Among other things Wright made the journal a live

newspaper, scoring several "beats" worthy of Bennett himself. In this he actively began to discuss life insurance. He found that the Mutual Benefit of New Jersey, recently organised, offered to insure by taking three-quarters of the premium in notes; and called it to account. He succeeded in persuading the officers of their mistake; had the satisfaction of being thanked by them for his criticism, and of seeing the Mutual Benefit develop into one of our greatest and best managed American companies. Wright called other companies to account for similar practices. He now went deeply into life-insurance mathematics. He decided, on his own hook, to prepare a series of actuarial tables—something then unknown in America. He worked for a year at his calculations; his own boys and girls set the type. It was published in 1853; a revised edition was issued in 1871 and is still considerably used. He eked out his living by translating La Fontaine's Fables—his translation still being preserved in all the bibliographies. All these years, however, Wright lived in the utmost poverty. At this time, too, he had a family of twelve children! His appearance on Boston Common, followed by his brood, was one of the sights of the times.

THE CAUSE OF ENGLAND'S SCANDALOUS RECORD

By this time, however, Elizur Wright had formulated his ideas as to needed reforms in life insurance.
He had carefully studied its scandalous history in
England, and had emphatically put his finger on the
cause. He found it in the endless opportunity offered
by the system itself. " I became persuaded," he said,
" that life insurance was the most available, convenient,
and permanent nidus for rogues that civilisation had
ever presented." No institution based upon general
benevolence, indeed, so contains within itself the possibilities of fraud. Theoretically devised to ameliorate
human suffering, its very structure is a constant temptation to the vicious. Ostensibly the life-insurance company merely collects certain sums from its members,
invests them at compound interest, and pays them back
as contracts mature. But there are two factors which
differentiate it from other financial institutions. The
first is the long period its policies run. The company
makes definite contracts for an indefinite time. It agrees
to pay stipulated sums, but to pay them only at death.
And the average life policy ·becomes a claim thirty
years after the first payment is made. Again, the company receives much larger amounts than the actual
insurance cost. This peculiarity results from the fact,

described in the first article, that men will not pay
for their insurance as they go. They will not pay its
actual cost this year, its actual cost next, and so on——
on the natural premium plan, that is—but insist on
paying the same amount each year—or a level premium. Consequently the companies attempt to average
up the yearly cost, and thus charge a greatly excessive
price in the early years, and a price much below cost in
the latter. They thus force the insured, during the
first half of the premium paying period, to *advance* a
considerable amount on the insurance cost of the latter
half. These advance payments, with accumulated interest, are the company's *reserves*. The Mutual Life, for
example, collects each year about $60,000,000 from its
policy-holders; but pays in death losses only about
$20,000,000. Its $40,000,000 balance, after deducting
expenses and other larger disbursements, is really the
advance payment of the insurance cost of succeeding
years; and this it *reserves* against the day when its
payment will be required. For such future payments
the Mutual Life has already heaped up some $440,-
000,000; and, even though it should cease writing new
policies to-day, this sum, so great is the accumulation
from compound interest, will in a few years increase
to $1,000,000,000.

In Wright's time these reserve premiums were a

constant temptation to plunder. The life companies assessed their premiums on the level payment, or part-advance payment, system, but were not legally held responsible for the great sums so accumulated. Being unrestrained by law, their officers could squander and steal these reserves and still maintain an outward show of solvency. They could, that is, for a considerable time, pay all their maturing claims. If they got in " new blood " and new cash they even more successfully concealed their crimes. In England, Wright found the life managers engaged in an unseemly scramble for these reserves. In the United States the New York and the Mutual Life drew upon their reserves to pay dividends. Recently Emory McClintock, the Mutual's actuary, declared that these dividends, if paid now, would be a signal for the sheriff.[1]

WRIGHT'S GREAT FIGHT FOR THE LEGAL RESERVE

Wright, apparently alone of all men in his generation, saw where this would end. He also pointed out the obvious remedy. He showed that the amounts deducted from each premium for reserve purposes were matters of precise mathematical calculation. Given a certain number of policies, of certain ages and fixed premiums, he

[1] Testimony before the Armstrong Investigating Com. Vol. III, page 2263.

could readily figure the total amount which must be laid aside each year. Very well, then why not pass a law requiring all companies to maintain this reserve? Why not place the enforcement of this law in the hands of an insurance commission which should make this annual calculation? Wright preached this reform with his usual enthusiasm. He was generally ridiculed and opposed. He was told that his scheme was impossible because of the enormous labour involved. Wright appeared before the Massachusetts legislature year after year, only to be jeered at and insulted. But he was one of those cranks who could not be browbeaten nor laughed down. He was engaged in what he regarded as a sacred task: " lobbying for the widow and orphan." And, almost by accident, his bill slipped through. He had been especially annoying all through the session of 1858. As usual, his gaunt figure and his remarkable mathematical discussions provoked only mirth. In those days, however, legislative courtesy prevailed almost as generally as now. It so happened that one member, who had been converted by Wright, had asked no favours that year. His friends finally rallied him about it. " Well, Fabens," they said, " you have asked nothing; what can we do for you? " Quick as a flash he answered: " Pass Wright's bill." In a moment the thing was done. Wright, who, as usual, was prowling around the state house in the interest of his favourite measure, quickly heard the news. He took the bill, rushed it over to the House, and, in the last few minutes of the session, that body hurried it through. Then Wright took it up to Governor Banks, and refused to leave his presence until the measure was signed.

In this haphazard fashion was American life insurance placed upon a solid basis. This was the beginning of the great modern life-insurance principle of the legal reserve. Wright's old abolitionist persistence, in the face of constant discouragement, redeemed the whole system in this country, popularised life insurance, made it one of the great safeguards of society, and saved millions of dollars to the beneficiaries of life-insurance policies. Not improbably he rescued from ultimate disaster such large companies as the Mutual and the New York Life, but, more than that, he gave American life insurance a standing unattained up to that time by that of any other country. He thus forced through a measure which has since been adopted by practically every state and territory. Wright made the failure of a life-insurance company mathematically impossible. No company which has observed the Massachusetts legal reserve law has ever gone to the wall. The financial stability of the three great New York companies, in spite of recent disclosures, has caused general amazement. The greatest banks, in the face of such assaults, would almost inevitably have landed in the receiver's hands. But the Equitable, the New York Life, and the Mutual have stood the awful tests of the last twelve months—and why? Simply because Elizur Wright, fifty years ago, "lobbied for the widow and orphan" in the Massachusetts legislature and thus made the life companies so strong that even the recent dishonest managements have not unsettled them. Thanks to Wright, life-insurance scandals to-day affect other things than the companies' solvency.

Greatly to Wright's surprise, he was himself selected as the first commissioner under this law. He had no right to anticipate the appointment, as he had no political qualifications. Governor Banks selected him, however, because he could find no one else to take the job. He picked out one or two political favourites, but they all refused. They could not undertake the monumental task involved, especially at the salary provided —$1500 a year. They all declared that there was only one man in Massachusetts who could enforce the law, and that was Elizur Wright.

AN OLD MAN AT AN OVERWHELMING TASK

The generation which has known the administrations of such insurance commissioners as our recent officials

in New York, may profitably study that of Elizur
Wright. Here was an insurance commissioner who took
his task seriously, who actually scrutinised life-insurance management, who had a wide conception of
official duty. In a little dingy room he laboured for
eight years over a mass of figures that would have
driven other men insane. He became an official interro-
gation point. He did not good-naturedly take the company's
pany's statements at their face value, but aroused their
ire by endlessly asking questions. There were thousands of things that he wished to know, most of them
consisting of that precise information which the companies were reluctant to give. How much money do you
take in each year? How much do you pay out? What
are your assets? In what form do you keep them?
Are your investments safe? What dividends do you
return? What salaries do you pay to your officers?
What commissions to your agents? How about this
item? How about that? He went to extremes to protect
the individual policy-holder. He prepared an amazing
volume which he called his " Life-Insurance Registry."
In this he kept a record of every policy issued by every
company doing business in Massachusetts. He had its
number, the amount of premiums paid, and the necessary reserve which should stand to its credit. He also
showed whether the companies had made this reserva-

tion, whether, in other words, they could pay the policy should it fall due. He invited all policy-holders to visit him for advice on this point. He thus entertained an endless procession; high and low constantly visited him. His attitude was paternal, almost patriarchal. He was already an old man, with a flowing white beard and white hair and a high bald head. As each policy-holder came before him, he consulted his bulky Registry and told him whether he was being cheated, how much he would lose by dropping his policy, and what the company was morally bound to pay on surrender. The amount of labour which went into these calculations is almost inconceivable. It was estimated that the work Wright did during his commissionership would have taken the average man eighty-two years. In one year he made 250,000 mathematical calculations. To facilitate this work he invented his famous Arithmeter, a calculating machine which is still extensively used.

AN INSURANCE COMMISSIONER WHO WAS A HUMAN INTERROGATION POINT

Wright, however, unlike many of his successors, did more than merely determine questions of solvency. Superintendent Hendricks has recently declared that his duties did not comprise general investigations of management; that its honesty or dishonesty did not primarily concern his department. If corruption were pointed out to him then he would properly take action; but he could not be expected to discover such things himself; he must be "told." For many years our life-insurance superintendents have examined the Mutual, the Equitable, and the New York Life, and have found nothing wrong. Mr. Hendricks, only three years ago, gave a clean bill of health to the Equitable. The great originator of state supervision did not so understand his task. He did not wait to have the evils pointed out; he thrust in his own probe and did not hesitate to publish what he found. He examined minutely each new company as it applied for admission into Massachusetts, and informed the public, in his official reports, whether it were good or bad. He did not quite like the investments of the John Hancock, and said so. He did not take kindly to the Equitable, organised in 1859. "Its surplus," he said, after making certain important deductions, "seems to belong to the stockholders." He found certain companies treating their retiring policy-holders unfairly, and mentioned them by name. He found others using too much money in current expenses, and published the facts broadcast. He went for the Massachusetts companies as vehemently as the rest. He found much stock jobbery in them. He discovered that, in certain companies, the stockholders had purchased their stock by "borrowing" the money from the company's surplus without interest; an old dodge of which there are many modern instances. By a refinement of rascality, they had lifted considerable sums out of the treasury, and then required the companies to pay them dividends on it. The one remedy, Wright declared, was to retire the stock altogether—to "mutualise"; and this the companies did. He found that other concerns solicited business on the promise of big dividends, and then refused to pay them. He made public all these facts in his annual reports. Of course the companies did not like this treatment. They called Wright's frankness, brutality. They accused him of furnishing ammunition to agents of rival companies. "Rose-water is good," Wright replied to one especially bitter onslaught, "but it never built pyramids or machine-shops. Before the temple is complete, we must have something besides frankincense." Meanwhile he discussed all life-insurance principles and problems as they have not been discussed before or since. His reports, written in beautiful and forcible English, are the greatest text-books extant on the subject. They became, in Wright's own lifetime, rare books; and have since been issued, so great has been the demand, in a special edition.

DISHONEST COMPANIES DRIVEN OUT OF MASSACHUSETTS

Wright, in his eight years' administration, drove fourteen dishonest companies out of Massachusetts. How he handled them is shown in his treatment of the American Mutual, of New Haven, and the International of London. His official honesty was especially tested in the case of the American Mutual. Its president was Prof. Benjamin Silliman, the great scientist of Yale, who had been Wright's beloved instructor in Natural Philosophy. Its active manager was one Benjamin Noyes—" Ben Noyes " he was popularly known —Silliman's son-in-law. Noyes is a picturesque figure in the life-insurance history of this country. Before Wright began his work his company did a flourishing business in Massachusetts. Wright applied his usual mathematical test and was far from satisfied. He found that Noyes was spending fifty cents out of every dollar he took in in " expenses "; that he had seriously impaired his reserves, and that his filed statements were absolutely false. Noyes daily committed the old sin of the English companies: he did not reserve the advance premiums of the early years, but used them in all sorts of extravagance. He insured everybody who offered, irrespective of their physical condition or employment

—in the mad chase for " new blood "; and annually contested half his claims. Wright therefore bodily threw his company out of Massachusetts. He boldly advised the American public to have nothing to do with it. He thus saved money for thousands of possible victims. In a few years the American Mutual went down, a riddled hulk; and the adventurous Benjamin Noyes wound up his career in state's prison.

At about the same time Wright directed his attention to the International of London. This was one of the most flourishing of the English life companies. It had several noblemen among its trustees; had, as its actuary, a Fellow of the Royal Astronomical Society. Its directors, like many of their modern successors, knew and cared little about the company and left its management to the executive officers. Wright soon found that they were running things chiefly in their own interest. Thomas Lamie Murray was the " founder " of the Society. He managed the company as a private graft. He organised it on the stock basis, but had only a small amount of this paid in. He had so phrased the charter that it fixed him in his place as chairman for life. He could not be removed even by the vote of the shareholders. In addition to his salary he had an agreement by which he received annually five per cent. of the " net profits "—this emolu-

ment also to be enjoyed by his heirs and assigns for
twenty-eight years after his death. Instead of reserving
his advance premiums, Murray used them constantly
in schemes of his own. He invested them in mines and
cheap stocks; lent them to his personal friends and
to his trustees. He used them to pay excessive agents'
commissions and travelling expenses—how modern this
all sounds! He did a fine business, however, and, just
before the inquisitive Wright came into office, congrat-
ulated his directors, in an official meeting, on the success of the American branch. Then Wright began to
ply him with questions. Would the International please
inform the Massachusetts Department concerning its
reserves? Had it laid by a sufficient sum to meet the
obligations of the future? Mr. Murray at first refused
to answer. " Very well," said Wright; " then withdraw
your agents from Massachusetts." Finally a report
was sent in. Wright found it a fine looking statement;
but it did not meet his dreary mathematical test. He
found that the International had a deficit of nearly
$1,000,000. He riddled the statement in his official re-
port, and was especially severe upon the distinguished
mathematicians that had countenanced it. " I find," he
said, " that there are parties connected with the parent
office in London who have endeavoured to deceive the
people of Massachusetts, making them believe that the

company has been earning large profits while it has really been squandering sacred funds. Its assets are only forty-seven cents on the dollar, and we should naturally think that no one could have known this better than a Fellow of the Royal Astronomical Society who had laboured four months over the figures." This report produced the most celebrated discussion in the history of American life insurance. The International called to its assistance the most distinguished actuaries in England, and Professor Pierce of Harvard, who twisted figures in every possible way to prove Wright in error. Again time justified Wright's action; again he kept the money of thousands of American policy-holders out of a mismanaged company. In about ten years the International found itself unable to pay its claims, because it had not kept proper reserves, and failed under scandalous conditions.

WRIGHT'S FIGHT IN BEHALF OF LAPSING POLICY-HOLDERS

Wright soon discovered that this legal reserve law did not reform the life-insurance business. It made life insurance safe and solvent; it did not make it just. It prevented companies from cheating their members out of their policy claims; it did not compel them to treat the insured fairly. Solvency, however, remarked

Wright, was not the only issue in life insurance; there was a question of equity as well. He found that the greatest abuses existed in the treatment of lapsing members. A few companies paid a certain surrender value on lapse; but, in the main, a system of wholesale forfeiture prevailed. Most policies stipulated the payment of premiums at certain dates, "twelve o'clock noon," on pain of absolute forfeiture. Policies were abandoned then, as they are now, in large numbers. In 1861 Wright found that six thousand two hundred and thirty-six policies had been terminated, and only six hundred and thirteen by death; the remaining five thousand six hundred and twenty-three, insuring $13,677,000, were dropped for non-payment of premium. Many of these were abandoned because of poverty. In other cases the reasons for insuring had passed. Hundreds were also dropped through inadvertence. Members forgot the day of payment, and would wake up, a week or so after, and find that the savings of years had been swept away. Stories are told of sea captains, who, detained on their voyages, returned to port to find their insurance suddenly wiped out. Illness, sudden insanity might also interfere with prompt payment.

The companies, of course, could not justify this on any sound life-insurance grounds. In all lapses the amount which they should return was pretty clearly indicated. It must be, of course, the larger part of the *reserve*. This reserve, as already explained, is the amount accumulated to meet future claims upon the policy; it provides, that is, for future contingencies. Manifestly, if a policy lapses, there can be no future contingencies to provide for; and clearly the accumulation should be returned. This principle is now generally recognised. If you lapse now, you get a considerable part of your reserve; if you borrow money from the company, that money is taken from your reserve. Before Elizur Wright pointed out this simple equity, few companies observed it. They all held large sums in their treasuries withheld from lapsing policyholders. Wright found that many companies encouraged the lapsing habit. In this way they obtained great sums which they used in wasteful expenditure. A peculiarity of the business, he pointed out, was that a company always enormously profited from its own bad reputation. Policy-holders were thus frightened into dropping out. Many unsound companies thus kept themselves from insolvency. They appropriated large parts of the premiums as they came in, and then recouped themselves by lapses. Many, like the Mutual Life of New York, paid all their working expenses in this way. In one year the New York Life made $375,-000 on lapses—in those days a large sum. In some cases swindlers obtained control of companies, and then spread the most damaging reports concerning their solvency. They sent agents broadcast to frighten policy-holders out, occasionally paying small sums on surrender. Then they themselves appropriated the money standing to the credit of the policies—that is, the reserves.

PASSAGE OF THE NON-FORFEITURE LAW

As far as the Massachusetts companies were concerned, Wright stopped all that. His law had clearly pointed out the nature of the reserve; and, as an essential corollary, he proposed another measure vesting its ownership in the insured. Thus, in 1861, Wright forced through the legislature, again in the face of united corporate opposition, his world-famous non-forfeiture law. This prevented the companies from appropriating, themselves, the reserves of their retiring members. Wright, at this time, did not compel them to pay the reserve back in cash; under this law, the companies, in case of lapse, applied it to continue the policies in force for the exact period the cash reserve would buy. The companies pressed the only valid argument ever brought against the surrender value: that it encouraged adverse selection against the company; that under it, only the healthy members would retire; that those

anticipating early death would certainly remain; and
that thus, by increasing the average of mortality, it
might weaken the company as a whole. Wright always
recognised the justice of this argument, as long as it
was not pushed to extremes; and so, in his first bill, he
allowed the companies to retain twenty per cent. of
the reserve as compensation for the loss of the member.
Afterward he regarded this *surrender charge* as excessive, and in other ways did not accept his own measure
as ideal. It marked, however, an epoch in life insurance. After 1861 no Massachusetts company could
cheat its retiring members. Though the law applied
only to Massachusetts it had a most wholesome influence
on life-insurance practice. The Massachusetts companies became so popular, because of their non-forfeiture features, that the system, more or less modified,
was generally adopted. From Wright's little dingy
room in Boston his non-forfeiture reform spread to
the four corners of the earth. England, whose companies had for generations robbed their retiring members, adopted the American system.

Wright next took up the subject which, more than
any other, has disturbed the life-insurance business for
the last twenty years—that of the surplus. As explained in a former article, life-insurance premiums are
purposely made redundant. The companies figure on a

certain amount for death claims, expenses, and reserves;
and then, to be on the safe side, always charge an excess price. This excess, when returned, is popularly
known as the " surplus " or " profits " or " dividends."
Wright found practically all companies returning their
surplus, or making their dividends, once in every five
years. They had borrowed this idea, as well as numerous
others, from England. Wright soon announced the
proper method; nearly fifty years ago he took a bold
stand for the annual dividend system. He declared
that it was a fault, rather than a source of pride, that
a company had large accumulations above the amount
required for its reserves. This simply signified that it
overcharged its insured; that it withheld from policy-
holders money which was rightfully their due. " If
the surplus should not be divided," he declared, " but
continue accumulating till those who are the first
contributors to it, and for that reason probably are
most largely interested, have dropped away by death,
or by the lapse or surrender of their policies, a wrong
will be done which, though not so frightful as bankruptcy, may be as extensive in its transfer of property
from the hands of owners into those of strangers."
At the beginning of Wright's administration few companies paid their dividends in cash, but in the form of
additional insurance. If the policy were lapsed, all these

paid-for additions were also forfeited. In this great reform, too, Wright's opinions ultimately prevailed. In
1866 the Mutual Life began to pay annual cash dividends. The other companies were forced by competition
to follow suit.

Wright was Commissioner from 1858 to 1867. In
those nine years he had entirely transformed the life-
insurance business. He developed the idea of state supervision, an idea now generally adopted. He made
American life-insurance companies the best in the
world. England readily admitted the superiority of
our system. In 1868 Gladstone devoted several days
to denouncing the practices of the English offices.
" Their proceedings," he said, " are worse than wholesale robbery, and there are many persons who have
never seen the inside of a gaol and yet who had better
be there than many a rogue that has been convicted
ten times over in the old Bailey. For needy aristocrats to make stool-pigeons of themselves is the regular game." At that time the American companies,
thanks to Wright's patient supervision, were our greatest national exemplars of honesty and justice. They
devoted themselves to a simple end—the insuring of
lives. Ninety per cent. of all their policies were on the
ordinary life plan. They had not discovered that life
insurance was an " investment." They knew nothing

about gold bonds. They distributed their surplus—paid their " dividends "—annually; they had no " deferred," no " accumulation " system; no tontines. They had no trust company annexes; did not use their funds generally in Wall Street; and did not make themselves adjuncts to great political parties. They furnished insurance, too, at much lower rates than the present quotations. They conducted business on a reasonable margin of expense. They paid only ten per cent. of the first premium to agents; now they pay anywhere from twenty-five to one hundred. They had no elaborate office buildings scattered all over the world. When the New York Life, in 1867, proposed to erect a modest structure on Broadway, several influential persons called upon the insurance department to suppress it on the ground of extravagance. American companies insured only Americans; they did not look for business in China and Japan.

DRIVEN OUT OF OFFICE; BUT A REFORMER STILL

Like all reformers, Wright paid the penalty of his zeal. He asked too many questions; demanded from the companies too many papers. He was too hard on the sharpers. His crowning sin was his exposure of the receivership proceedings of the Eagle Insurance Company. He found the receivers milking this dry, and in

his usual blunt fashion published the facts. His enemies combined against him. " Ben " Noyes, whose
company he had driven out of Massachusetts, worked
night and day to unseat him. Wright, being no poli-
tician, knew nothing of all this, and while he busily
pored over his figures, the politicians at the state
house deftly legislated him out of office.

Though thus summarily removed from an influential
position, Wright by no means gave up the battle for
honest life insurance. He was now sixty-four years old ;
but he had the fiercest struggle of his life before him.
New York now began to get the lead as the headquarters or life insurance ; had begun to develop the
dishonest practices which, in their full flower, have
recently been revealed. Henry B. Hyde had started his
great Tontine scheme ; William H. Beers had followed
suit in the New York Life ; and the Winston régime
had gained the upper hand of the Mutual. These forces
combined to undo practically everything that Wright
had done. He had built up life insurance on the basis
of honest state supervision ; they did all they. could,
by corrupting the departments, to undo it. He had
rid life insurance in part of its greatest evil—that of
forfeitures ; they proceeded to recast the whole life-
insurance system with forfeitures as its keystone. He
had induced a period of mangement economy ; they in-

stituted the present extravagance. He had made life insurance an institution run entirely in the interest of the insured; they reduced it to a machine run, as Wright himself phrased it, " chiefly in the interest of the runners." Against all these innovations, of course, Wright took a firm stand. From his home at Medford he almost daily, for twenty-five years, inveighed against what he called the " New York life-insurance ring." Almost alone, he foresaw many things that Mr. Charles E. Hughes has recently laid bare; he even exposed many of the particular abuses which, in the last few months, have so astounded the public. His strictures on the Mutual and Equitable read almost as though written yesterday.

WRIGHT'S LONG BATTLE WITH THE MUTUAL LIFE

And it is not until we study his twenty-five years' campaign that we realise how long-seated are the present evils; how frequently they, and even the very men recently in control, have been exposed; how really short-lived the public memory is; and how great the danger is that, because of this national forgetfulness, the present upheaval may not end in lasting reform. Especially instructive, from this standpoint, is Elizur Wright's long battle with the Mutual Life. About 1869 he discovered the corrupting influences at work. Fred-

erick S. Winston had organised a palace revolution
and seated himself in control. Winston was a bankrupt dry-goods merchant. For several years he drew
no stated stipend from the Mutual Life, but received
irregular " advances." His creditors had hauled him
up in supplementary proceedings; and he evidently
adopted this arrangement to keep his salary from
them.[2] Winston was a man of commanding energy,
of despotic and choleric temper; short, stout, dignified
—the very type of high-toned financier always inevitably associated with the Mutual Life. He was a trustee
in five or six churches, connected with the American
Bible Society, and deeply interested in foreign missions. Robert H. McCurdy had been closely associated
with him for many years; and naturally when the
latter's son, Richard A., was graduated from Harvard, a place was readily found for him in the Mutual
Life. Wright soon discovered that Winston and Mc-
Curdy were managing the Mutual in the most high-
handed fashion. They ignored their trustees, except a
favoured inside ring, to whom special favours were
granted, precisely as the great life-insurance managements do now. " Dummy directors " was already a
phrase in current use. They had already fully developed

[2] Ebenezer Dale against Frederick S. Winston, Supreme Court
of the State of New York. A. B. Tappan, Referee. Oct. 1865.

the present system of proxy control. The Mutual Life, and all the other mutual companies, had been organised as pure democracies. They had no shareholders, the theory being that the policy-holders would elect, by a general plebiscite, the trustees and equally participate in all the benefits of the business. Winston and McCurdy, declared Elizur Wright, had transformed their company into a pure autocracy. They held proxies enough, he said, to insure their own election, in " the face of any opposition, short of the miraculous." In fact, they had twenty thousand or thirty thousand ready to vote at the slightest indication of revolt. They jocularly called these proxies their " children of Israel," because they were too numerous to count. They publicly announced their purpose of selecting only those trustees " who were friendly to themselves," and rode rough-shod over any independent policy-holders' movement. Back in 1869 several New York members attempted to unseat them. This election resembled a Sixth ward primary. As a measure of intimidation, the Mutual compelled all policy-holders to write their names on the back of their ballots. The leader of the opposition was violently assailed by an administration " watcher," who threatened, in so many words, to " smash his face." In the end, after a few timid policy-holders had deposited their votes, McCurdy came up and dumped several hundred proxies into the box; and so, easily carried the day. That was the last time the policy-holders ever tried to control the Mutual.[3]

Under Winston many present-day abuses—nepotism, legislative corruption, improper use of policy-holders' funds, and illiberal treatment of the insured—first got their start. The executive officers carefully safeguarded their own interests. They all received the most liberal salaries and, at the end of each year, voted themselves additional " bonuses." In three years they thus added $189,000 to their regular compensation. In order to conceal this transaction, they charged these amounts as *dividends to policy-holders*.[4] Winston had quartered upon the Mutual's agency force numerous relatives. He had one son as Medical Examiner, another as cashier, another as clerk. He had appointed his son-in-law, one Harvey B. Merrill, to the Mutual's most lucrative general agency. Merrill had his headquarters at Detroit, and received a percentage on every

[3] Testimony of the Committee on Grievances relative to the petition of Stephen English (1873 New York Assembly Document 169, page 108).

[4] For corroboration of this charge, see Report of the Committee relative to the petition of Stephen English. New York Assembly Document No. 155; 1873: "The distribution of a bonus of over $189,000 among the officers of the Company, in addition to their ample salaries, and its concealment from the policy-holders by charging far the greater portion of it to *dividend account*, were proved to be true."

policy written in the states of Michigan, Indiana, Illinois, Wisconsin, and Minnesota. Winston himself admitted, on the witness-stand, that while enjoying these perquisites Merrill spent a considerable part of his time in Europe.[5] The gross income of his agency amounted to more than $100,000[6] a year. In 1865 President Winston's son, Frederick M., died. He had taken out policies to the extent of $12,000, but, several years before his death, had surrendered them for their cash values. The Insurance Committee revived these policies and paid the $12,000 to young Winston's widow.[7] Judge Alexander Bradford, a Mutual trustee—one of the inner ring—had held for several years a $10,000 policy, but had surrendered it. When Bradford was on his deathbed the Mutual restored it.[8] Winston also extended improper favours to a few

[5] Examination of witnesses before George W. Miller, 1870, Page 242.

[6] From this amount, of course, must be deducted the commissions paid to sub-agents.

[7] Report of the Committee on Grievances relative to the petition of Stephen English (1873 New York Assembly Document 155): "The charge that surrendered and forfeited policies in the life of President Winston's son had been revived, *after his death*, was proved to be true." Page 3.

[8] Ibid: page 3. "The illegal purchase, at a higher rate than its surrender value, of a policy on the life of a trustee; its subsequent restoration when he was actually moribund and its payment as a death claim, was proved."

inside trustees. He deposited money in banks in which certain trustees were interested. He also lent money to others under suspicious circumstances. He thus advanced $30,000 to Seymour L. Husted, on the pretence of purchasing United States bonds. When Husted paid it back Winston, in order to conceal the transaction from the trustees, compelled a clerk to falsify the accounts.[9] He lent $18,000 to certain state commissioners, and carried it on the books as " cash on hand." He farmed out the business of examining titles on mortgage real estate loans to favoured trustees. Under his régime also the use of Mutual money for legislative purposes began. In an investigation into the Mutual Life, held in 1870, President Winston admitted that he had given a well-known lawyer $6000 for work at Albany in connection with certain proposed legislation.[10] This appeared in the Mutual's books as " taxes." " This lawyer earned the money," added Winston. The Mutual also admitted paying $3500 to George W. Miller, Superintendent of Insurance, to further a bill intended to crush out smaller rivals. These items may seem small compared with recent lavish expendi-

[9] Examination of witnesses before George W. Miller, Superintendent of Insurance in relation to certain charges against the trustees and officers of the Mutual Life Insurance Co. (1870). Pages 82-83.

[10] Ibid: page 237.

tures for similar purposes; but there is the germ of present-day Houses of Mirth and Andrew Hamiltons.

In the great scandal which shook the Mutual to its foundation thirty-five years ago and resulted in the deposition of Sheppard Homans as actuary, Elizur Wright himself had played a part. In 1869 Homans refused to audit President Winston's financial statement. He declared that it contained gross inaccuracies. He pointed to an item of $2500 charged up as rent for the Boston office, which had really been paid to Henry B. Hyde, president of the Equitable, for legislative purposes at Albany. IIe also declared that President Winston proposed to deprive his policyholders of a large amount of *post-mortem* dividends. The Mutual was then on the annual dividend system. In case a member died his beneficiary received, with the full claim, the amount of the next succeeding dividend. Winston, without consulting the trustees, declared that these should no longer be paid. Homans, the actuary, insisted that they should. A fine row resulted. Winston acted in his usual arbitrary fashion. He told Homans that if he didn't certify to the statement, he would get another actuary who would; and, in fact, finally compelled Homans' assistant to put his name to it. The trustees were finally aroused, however, and referred the question to Elizur Wright and two

other experts. Wright declared that the dividends
must be paid. Winston still refused, and dismissed Homans for insubordination. Afterward, Homans frequently declared, the Mutual had to appropriate $2,-
000,000 to rectify this mistake.

WRIGHT ESTABLISHES THE CASH SURRENDER SYSTEM

Wright made Winston's existence unbearable for
fifteen years. He exposed injustices of the insurance
system he stood for. He riddled his annual reports,
showing, year after year, how the financial statements
were twisted. He particularised extravagance practically identical with those which the recent investigation
has disclosed. He declared that the Mutual staff divided
each year at least $150,000 of superfluous salary.
Again and again he called attention to the wasteful-
ness of the agency department. This then, as now, was
a portentous scandal. Wright also showed that the
Mutual spent enormous sums for advertising. It sub-
sidised, by advertisements, not far from thirty life-
insurance papers; and had also largely muzzled the
daily press. Much indignation has been aroused by
recent revelations of the Mutual's publicity bureau;
its collection of journalistic leeches; of " Dollar-a-
line " Smith, whose business it was to secure favourable notices of the Mutual and its officers. Elizur

Wright exposed all that thirty years ago. He frequently found it impossible to get his own communications in the papers because of the Mutual's influence. Attacks upon him frequently appeared in the New York papers, sometimes printed as extracts from other journals. Wright learned that these had been paid for at the now familiar rate of a dollar a line!

Wright's greatest struggle with the Mutual was in his attempt to establish a system of cash surrender values. He began this agitation in 1869, and kept at it for nearly eleven years. He always had the utmost solicitude for those compelled to lapse their policies. He soon became dissatisfied with his 1861 non-forfeiture law. It granted only extended insurance; Wright insisted that the companies must, if required, pay cash. He clearly demonstrated the reasonableness of this. He took the position that the reserve on each policy—the advanced payment, the unearned premium —belonged exclusively to the insured. He was entitled, Wright declared, to do whatever he wished with it. If he wished to borrow it, the company must lend; if he wished to leave the company and take the larger part of it with him, he could do so. In 1871 he introduced his cash surrender law in the Massachusetts legislature. He got it through the House, but Judge McCurdy came up in the interest of the Mutual and killed it in the Senate. The Mutual fought it because it made enormous profits on lapses. It treated its retiring policy-holders with the utmost illiberality. It had no fixed rule; if one wished to surrender his policy, he got just what the company saw fit to give; if he lapsed, nothing at all. Under no condition did the Mutual ever pay more than fifty per cent. Wright showed that the Mutual had lapsed more than fifty per cent. of all the policies issued; and that it thus mulcted policy-holders of $1,000,000 a year. In 1876 he attempted to get in the Massachusetts legislature in order to fight for cash surrender values, but failed. Ultimately, however, he won his great fight. In 1880 Massachusetts passed Wright's cash surrender bill. All companies have adopted his ideas; cash values and loans are now written in nearly every policy issued. The New York companies make more noise over their cash surrender features than any others—entirely forgetful of the viciousness with which they opposed them for years. The Mutual, which, in Wright's time, gave only a small part of the reserve on surrender, now loudly boasts that it gives more.

Wright's denunciations of the Equitable now have all the sanctity of prophecy. He had a certain admiration for Henry B. Hyde as a pushing life-insurance man, but abhorred his practices. He denounced the Ton-

HENRY B. HYDE AT 22

came Hyde, who, by introducing numerous innovations, proceeded to deform the whole institution.

In those early Mutual Life days Henry B. Hyde was one of the handsomest and most promising young men in New York. Health and energy had written themselves in his every feature. He stood more than six feet high; was big-boned and strong-limbed—a splendid type of physical man. A keen and observant mind was reflected in piercing black eyes, partly hidden under dark overhanging eyebrows; determination and audacity were indicated in a square-jawed mouth, with an occasional play of harsh humour in the corners. He had persuasive manners and undoubted "magnetism"; enjoyed a certain popularity with the Mutual Life policy-holders, with whom he frequently came in contact; and by his office associates had already been marked out for success. Even then, however, Hyde was a good deal of a rattle-brain; he talked loudly and constantly, and frequently manifested more interest in certain grandiose plans of his own than the humdrum duties of his position. He had little sympathy with the go-as-you-please methods then prevailing in life insurance. Striding up and down the office, he would entertain his associates with descriptions of what the Mutual, under energetic management, might become. Some day, he intimated, he might himself take a hand in this life-

insurance game; already he had dreams of a new company, which, by using more aggressive methods, might
equal, perhaps surpass, the Mutual Life itself. Then,
clapping his hat on his head, he would rush madly
down Broadway. In an hour or two he usually returned
with an application for life insurance in his pocket.
Indeed, even then he spent a considerable part of his
time soliciting insurance. Already he had acquired some
local reputation as a hustling agent.

A FAMOUS LIFE-INSURANCE TRIO

From his earliest days Hyde seemed destined to
a life-insurance career. He was born at Catskill,
New York, in 1834, the son of a small country merchant. He had limited educational opportunities, and,
at sixteen, found it necessary to shift for himself.
As a boy he lingered wistfully around the dock at
Catskill, whence the boats regularly sailed to New
York—his highest ambition, a voyage to the " great
city." Into his father's home, in the late forties, perco-
lated a considerable assortment of life-insurance literature. The great mutual companies had recently started
in Massachusetts and New York; and Hyde, as a child,
spent many long winter evenings over the circulars
and letters they scattered broadcast. What " Robinson
Crusoe " and " Gulliver's Travels " are to most grow-

ing boys, were these crude advertising appeals to the
youthful Hyde. In his enthusiasm the child received
much encouragement and instruction from his old
schoolmaster, one John C. Johnston, and from his
father, Henry Hazen Hyde. For several years the three
talked and thought of nothing else. Johnston finally
abandoned his school and became an active agent for the
Mutual Life. Henry Hazen Hyde followed his example.
Both men met with such success that, in 1850, they
determined on a wider field. Taking young Henry B.
Hyde with them—he had just turned his sixteenth year
—they started for New York. The departure of that
trio from the village of Catskill marks an epoch in
the history of American life-insurance. In a few years
Henry Hazen Hyde became the most successful agent
in the United States. He had that same fluency of
speech, that same earnestness in persuasion, that same
strength against discouragement which afterward carried his son to such unparalleled success. He also
originated many of the agency methods which Henry
B. Hyde afterward so effectively used. He ultimately
built up a business at Boston that yielded him an income of $20,000 a year. Schoolmaster Johnston had
an even more remarkable career. After spending several
years in the service of the Mutual Life he went West
and, in 1858, helped found a company which has since

become the Northwestern Mutual of Milwaukee. Henry
B. Hyde found no immediate opening in life insurance,
and, perforce, accepted an uncongenial clerkship in a
mercantile house. In a year or two, however, he obtained,
through his father's increasing influence, a minor position with the Mutual Life.

A " PROXY ELECTION " IN 1853

In properly estimating Hyde's career we must give
due consideration to the moral atmosphere in which
his apprenticeship was spent. The office of the Mutual
Life, even as far back as the early fifties, could hardly
be regarded as a training-school for high business
ideals. Indeed, the recently deposed McCurdy-Winston
dynasty first got its clutches on the Mutual in 1853,
and thus enjoyed an unbroken succession of more than
half a century. Young Hyde had hardly obtained his
minor clerkship when the first great Mutual scandal
upset the town. Organised as a mutual company in
1843, it maintained this character for less than ten
years. In the early fifties one of its trustees, Frederick
S. Winston, discovered that method of controlling
mutual companies which now so generally prevails.
Every Mutual policy-holder had a vote for trustees,
and in those early days, when the company was small,
did pretty generally exercise this suffrage. Winston,

JOHN C. JOHNSTON   JOSEPH B. COLLINS

FREDERICK S. WINSTON

who was weak financially, decided to obtain proxies sufficient to secure his own election. To this end he associated himself with Robert H. McCurdy and several other leading merchants in the dry-goods trade. They enlisted also as proxy collector the services of John C. Johnston, who had now become the leading Mutual Life agent in New York City, and closely identified himself with the Winston party in the board of trustees.

In three years Johnston collected a sufficient number of proxies to elect seven new Winston-McCurdy trustees; and, at a snap meeting held in 1853, Joseph B. Collins, the president, was deposed and Winston put in. The new management promptly voted $35,000 to Johnston—all under the guise of buying up an agency contract. For several years a bitter warfare existed among the trustees. In 1855 Joseph Blunt, the Mutual's counsel and a leading anti-Winston man, formally presented to the Board charges of mismanagement against the Winston régime. With the circumstances changed, and giving due consideration to the comparative smallness of the Mutual Life, there is a striking similarity to conditions recently revealed. Thus the Mutual's Board is now largely made up of financiers; and the recent investigation demonstrated the use of its money in Wall Street enterprises. In 1855 its Board was largely made up of dry-goods merchants; and then,

according to Blunt, its funds were regularly used in
the dry-goods trade. "Loans upon dry-goods paper,"
he declared, commonly figured among its assets. There
was only one member of the finance committee, said
Blunt, who had not borrowed from the company.
Blunt also called attention to the "enormous and
rapidly increasing expenses of the company"; and
also charged that the trustees and officers took commissions on policies. Blunt's accusations caused considerable commotion, and there was even talk of a
legislative investigation. Unquestionably Henry B. Hyde
was an interested spectator.

Through all these early years Hyde kept constantly
at work at his great scheme—the organisation of a
new life-insurance company. He had rooms at Irving
Place and Fifteenth Street; and here, every evening,
after his work in the Mutual office, he entertained his
incredulous friends with descriptions of his forthcom-
ing enterprise. Among these early friends was Mr.
James W. Alexander—the recently deposed president
of the Equitable—then a junior at Princeton College.
Hyde had already joined the Fifth Avenue Presbyterian
Church, of which young Alexander's father was the
pastor, and had particularly displayed enthusiasm as
a worker in the Y. M. C. A. He constantly buttonholed
the influential members of Dr. Alexander's congrega-

tion in the interest of his proposed company. His propaganda was not unqualifiedly successful. His associates
in the Mutual office ridiculed his enthusiasm; his older
friends pointed out the difficulties in his way. The
insurance law of 1853 required a capital stock of
$100,000 in all new insurance companies. How, Hyde's
friends asked him, could a young man, without high
social or financial influence, secure as large a sum as
that? Hyde, however, had one supporter and one be-
liever: his father, Henry Hazen Hyde, who frequently
attended those preliminary conferences in his son's
rooms and, in several substantial ways, assisted him in
his enterprise.

HYDE DISMISSED FROM THE MUTUAL

Now Hyde sought encouragement in another source
—the Mutual Life office itself. In those days the Mutual
would write only $10,000 on a single life, and con-
sequently its agents had to take many applications
elsewhere. Why, thought Hyde, should not his new
company get this excess business? So one cold March
night in 1859 he called upon Frederick S. Winston at
his home. His reception was not cordial. Winston, of
course, had already learned of his scheme; and that anyone, especially a Mutual employee, should contemplate
founding a rival company he regarded as little less

than an impertinence. He informed Hyde that he did not favour the scheme; and, that, moreover, anyone even meditating such a plan could not retain his position with the Mutual Life. Hyde met this defiance in the proper spirit, and asked how soon his resignation could be accepted.

"You can call at the office Monday morning and deliver your keys and cash," replied Winston. "It will not take the actuaries long to examine your accounts."

And, with that, he shut the door on his presumptuous young cashier. That brief interview tremendously affected the history of American life insurance. Forgiveness was not Henry B. Hyde's most striking characteristic; and the behaviour of Frederick S. Winston, on this occasion, he never forgot. Winston himself little imagined how much humiliation and annoyance he had thus prepared for himself. Hyde had originally intended to work, in a measure, at least, in co-operation with the Mutual; now he exerted all his energies to crushing it. For years he pursued Winston and his company, got millions of business that would naturally have gone to it, and ultimately wrested from it its leadership in American life insurance. The one striking fact in the life-insurance situation for the last fifty years has been the rivalry and hatred existing between these two companies. Even now a Mutual official bristles whenever the Equitable is mentioned; and to a loyal Equitable man the Mutual's name is still anathema. Winston, always ungenerous and unscrupulous, at once began his attacks. He even refused Hyde a letter of honourable dismissal, and went personally to the young man's backers in the Fifth Avenue Presbyterian Church, advising them to have nothing to do with young Hyde or his company. Hyde was organising it, he declared, only for the purpose of selling out to the Mutual.

THE ERA OF COMPETITION BEGINS

Hyde returned the attack in kind. He called the succeeding Monday morning, delivered up his keys and cash, and formally took his leave. Then he quietly rented a back room on the second floor of the very building in which the Mutual had its office! " It was a matter of sentiment with me," he frequently said, " to have my office directly over that of the Mutual Life." He borrowed a table and a few chairs, and placed a box of cigars on the mantelpiece, to give an air of congeniality and comfort. Then he had painted a huge sign, " The Equitable Life Assurance Society," in large white letters on a black background. He hung this directly over the Mutual's less conspicuous sign, making it appear almost ridiculous by contrast. In this one episode Hyde clearly revealed his own character and his future policy. Herein he displayed his abounding confidence in himself and his own destiny; he had no company, no money, no stockholders, no charter, no legal right to the " Equitable's " name, which he thus bravely emblazoned. He had not even a single promise of support! His act in thus beginning business with no legal warrant is paralleled by numerous other happenings in his after career. Again he thus inaugurated that era of competition, always feverish and frequently unscrupulous, which has continued up to the present time and had such unfortunate consequences for the insured. Hyde, from the first, regarded the life-insurance field as his peculiar province. He started in to monopolise it, to wage war upon his rivals wherever they appeared. He regarded every company as a natural enemy; but above all, he selected the Mutual Life, because of its existing leadership, and because of his rough treatment in the early days, as his especial mark. Up to that time the mildest competition had prevailed, but since that March morning in 1859, when Henry B. Hyde hung his Equitable sign directly over the Mutual's, life insurance in this country has been an unremitting battle.

The episode illustrates another marked Hyde characteristic: his instinct for an advertisement. The onslaught of this unborn pygmy upon the Mutual giant was soon the talk of the town. Unquestionably it assisted Hyde in the important task in hand—the raising of that $100,000 capital stock. For several weeks Hyde canvassed influential New York. Few rich men successfully avoided his advances. He enlisted many supporters in the Fifth Avenue Presbyterian Church. He corralled others by promising them important positions in his society. He offered to make Dr. Edward W. Lambert medical director, provided he raise $25,000 of capital stock; and to make Henry Day counsel, provided he raised a similar amount. He showed his shrewdness by providing for a Board of fifty-two directors. He thus secured support and influence in many directions; and also a large number of initial policy-holders. He insisted that all directors show their confidence by insuring their own lives—a wise precedent, which has not been generally followed. Hyde himself obtained, from other sources, a large amount of insurance. In company with Dr. Lambert, he solicited business from door to door. Hyde, obtaining a prospective client, at once turned him over to the doctor for examination. Thus, before they left the candidate's presence they were prepared to issue the policy. New York, in those early days, was not accustomed to these rapid-fire methods, and Hyde and Lambert did not always receive respectful consideration. "We were never actually kicked out," said the doctor later, "but unquestionably there were times when discretion saved us." When the Equitable opened its doors on June 1, 1859, Hyde had nearly $500,000 of insurance on the books.

Hyde made every show of respectability. He started his institution, as we have seen, amid an ecclesiastical environment. He also took Mr. William C. Alexander, a professional and social star, brother of the Fifth Avenue pastor, as his president. He had at first intended the presidency for himself, but quickly recognised the business advantage of an older and more conservative man. He carefully selected one, however, whom he could control. He relegated himself to the apparently subordinate position of vice-president, but from the first kept the active management in his own hands. He calmly appropriated as his company's name that of the "Equitable Assurance Society of London," the most conspicuous in the world. He chiefly depended for public confidence, however, upon his assertion that the Equitable was a "purely mutual" company. He had capital stock indeed; and the majority of this capital stock has always controlled the society; but that capital stock was a requirement of the state law. In 1859

you couldn't organise a mutual company in New York
State. No law has more adversely affected life-insurance history. It created, in a dozen years, some forty-
one stock companies, all, like the Equitable, with at
least $100,000 capital. Of these only eleven survived.
Most of the others—the Continental, the Guardian, the
Widows and Orphans, the North America, the Universal, the American Popular—fell into the hands of
financial buccaneers who, in the seventies and early
eighties, repeated in New York State all the old English scandals. Hyde overcame the difficulty, however, by
the pretence of apportioning the earnings of the company not among the stockholders, but the insured. At
an early organisation meeting he loudly denounced
certain wicked shareholders who wished to obtain more
than the legal rate of interest on their investment.
They timidly suggested ten instead of seven per cent.
"Gentlemen," declared Hyde, shaking with wrath, "I
have made up my mind that this shall be a purely
mutual company, and if this provision, limiting the
dividends on the capital to legal interest, is not put
into the charter, I will take my hat and walk out of
this room and shall have nothing further to do with
the enterprise." He was at that time twenty-five years
old; his shareholders represented much of the wealth
and venerability of New York. The guilty ones, how-

ever, were silenced, and Hyde was given a free rein to inaugurate his philanthropy on the purely mutual basis. From the first, Hyde unblushingly insisted upon this point. He always officially declared that the Equitable was purely "mutual"; and kept carefully concealed from public view his capital stock. In the interests of economy and strict mutuality, he also fixed his president's salary at $1500 a year. He placed his own at the same modest figure; but this, as we shall see, had an interesting string to it.

Hyde started the Equitable with a definite programme in mind. Most life-insurance companies were then making very leisurely progress. They didn't get more business, Hyde declared, simply because they did not go after it. They waited for it to come to them. They did not hunt it on the highways, did not pursue it in every office and at every hearth. The possibilities of an aggressive agency system they little understood. Agents at that time hardly received enough to justify men in giving their undivided attention to the work. Many companies paid only five or ten per cent. of the first premium. Hyde had a theory that by increasing these commissions he could attract more aggressive men. He thus proposed to build up a great corporation, with the hustling agent as the fulcrum. From the first Hyde was never anything more than a great life-insurance agent, the greatest getter of new business the world has ever known. In the highest sense he was not a life-insurance man at all. Of its technicalities he knew little and cared less. We search his reports in vain for those enlightened discussions of life-insurance problems which illumine the papers of Jacob L. Greene and Amzi Dodd; his only thought was not how to improve conditions for his policy-holders, but how he might get more. He did not regard life insurance primarily as a great co-operative scheme for relieving human distress, but as a business. To get this business he sacrificed everything: honesty, the interest of the insured, even at times the stability of his company. He boasted openly that his aim was not to make the Equitable the best insurance company, but the largest.

EVOLUTION OF THE MODERN LIFE-INSURANCE AGENT

Thus, from the very first, he manifested the keenest interest in the agency department. The dry routine he left to others; the direct solicitation of new business he must supervise himself. He became the active leader of the Equitable's forces in the field. He started with only two agents and an office-boy, but before the Civil War began he had more than two hundred men actively at work. Nearly all of these he appointed himself. He

showed the life-insurance plodder, for the first time,
what generous treatment meant. He not only paid his
men well, but showed consideration in other ways. He
encouraged them to visit him, and never, even to the
end, refused to see the humblest worker on his staff.
He would frequently keep bank presidents cooling their
heels in an outer office while he entertained a favourite
" producer." He treated his successful solicitors with
ten times the deference he showed his pompous trustees.
" Directors are easy enough to get," he once informed
his Board to its own face; " what I want are hustling
agents." He had absolutely no dignity where they were
concerned. Somewhat morose and distant with most
men, with his active field force he was congeniality
itself. A good application was usually rewarded with a
hearty slap on the back; a large month's business was
always recognised by a congratulatory telegram. He
frequently entertained his men at dinner, and constantly corresponded with them. All advertising matter,
all pamphlets, he supervised and usually prepared himself. He early adopted the practice of circularising his
force at regular intervals. His famous " hints " to
agents, issued in 1865, is still a classic in life-insurance
literature.

If you wish to trace the evolution of the modern life-
insurance agent, you will find it in this little compen-

dium. Hyde herein imagines every situation in which his agent might find himself, and furnishes precise instructions for meeting it. There is only one way to "get business," he declares: unwearied personal canvass. Make use of all your friends and associates. Get lists from your doctor of insurable people, and, if necessary, make it an inducement to him to smooth the way. Make your clergyman help you insure his flock; join literary societies and clubs—in order that you may insure the members. When you are in company note carefully all manifestly interested in the subject, and call upon them the succeeding day. Follow up every marriage and every funeral. What better wedding present than a life-insurance policy? What more persuasive argument than the death of a man uninsured? Detailed and separate instructions are given for canvassing tradesmen, professional men, merchants, and every other social class. "You will find," said Hyde, thus forecasting the modern attitude of cynicism toward the policy-holder, "that nineteen men out of twenty will let you decide for them." Hyde pursued his own agents as unceasingly as he advised them to pursue the public. While his dignified competitors took things easy in their New York offices he was whirling all over the United States, everywhere strengthening and inspiring the Equitable force. One week he dropped in on the Boston office; the next he appeared unexpectedly at Philadelphia; a few days later at Chicago. He was always ready to lend a helping hand; always at the beck and call of any agent handling a difficult " case." In such contingencies he would himself visit the prospective candidate—and almost invariably with success. In more tangible ways he encouraged his men. He early inaugurated the custom of offering prizes for unusually meritorious work. Gold watches, silver pitchers, and salvers exuded from the Equitable office even forty years ago. He made bets with his agents as to the amount of business they could or could not do in a certain time. He liked to pit one successful man against another. Hyde himself became the agents' ideal; his men fairly idolised him. He early gave the Equitable that reputation, which it enjoyed for many years, as the " agents' company." " Here lies the friend of life-insurance agents," an Equitable after-dinner orator once proposed as a suitable epitaph for Henry B. Hyde.

" STEALING AGENTS "

In the earliest days Hyde participated in that pleasing life-insurance practice now generally known as " stealing agents." He raided in particular the field forces of the Mutual and the New York Life. He pounced upon their shining lights wherever they appeared, and tempted them away by unheard-of commission rates. He had no fixed schedules; he paid precisely what, in the individual case, the circumstances justified. "I have no rule that I will not break" he frequently declared. A single episode illustrates his methods. In the early sixties the New York Life's most successful agent was one A. W. Russell, of Boston. At that time commission rates ranged from fifteen to twenty-five per cent. of the first premium, and about seven per cent. on renewals. Hyde offered Russell fifty per cent. of the first premium and ten per cent. on renewals. Mr. Theodore M. Banta, in behalf of the New York Life, appealed to William Barnes, Superintendent of Insurance of New York State, for protection against such outrageous competition. Mr. Barnes sent for Hyde, warned him that such methods must end in bankruptcy, and virtually ordered him to keep his hands off Russell. Hyde stormed about the office, pounded the desk, and told the Superintendent that he should pay his agents whatever compensation he chose. "Suppose I should publish in to-morrow's *Tribune*," replied Mr. Barnes, "that the Equitable is doing business upon plans which I think disastrous?" Hyde still declared that he should manage the Equitable according to his own ideas. Mr. Banta

then rushed up to Boston to lay the situation before
Elizur Wright. Then Hyde capitulated. "While I
was sitting on the piazza waiting for Mr. Wright,"
said Mr. Banta years afterward, recalling the episode,
"Mr. Hyde drove up, and said that he would drop the
matter."[1] Though foiled in this particular case, Hyde
succeeded in numerous others.

"Stealing agents" has since become an indispensable talent of a successful life-insurance manager, and
one of the chief causes for the increase in the cost of
life insurance.

In five or six years the Equitable thus assembled
what was unquestionably, judged by certain standards,
the ablest agency force then at work. And its greatest and most successful agent was Henry Baldwin
Hyde himself. He not only told his subordinates how
to get the business; he showed, by his own example,
how it could be done. He gave his days and nights to
the society. He bustled into the office at an early hour.
"How many new applications?" was always his first
feverish inquiry. He spent the morning over his cor-
respondence, usually with Equitable agents, in prepar-
ing circulars and advertising matter, and receiving

---

[1] Testimony of Theodore M. Banta before the Trustees of the
Mutual Life, in the examination of charges against William H.
Beers (p. 344 et seq., manuscript copy).

callers. Casual droppers-in seldom got away from Hyde's office without signing applications for insurance, and usually leaving checks for the first premium. Hyde spent his afternoons and evenings personally soliciting insurance. He joined the ranks and worked side by side with the humblest agent. In every citizen he saw a prospective policy-holder. He utilised all his business associates; he made every one insure with whom he or the society did business. He forced in his banker, his butcher, his barber, his tailor. He would stop strangers on Broadway and discourse on the advantages of an Equitable policy. "How well I remember," years afterward said Luther R. Marsh, "when, on a blustering March morning in 1860, a gentleman, then unknown to me, came into my office and attempted to effect an insurance on my life. The visitor was one whose countenance was a letter of introduction and whose presence and manner commanded attention. I listened; my prejudice melted away; my arguments were answered; and the result was that a $10,000 policy was issued that afternoon. That visitor was Henry B. Hyde." Hyde met endless difficulties and discouragements. He could hardly have started his company at a more inopportune time; he had barely completed its organisation when the Civil War began and hard times set in. Hyde, however, kept valiantly on. In the earlier years, when the force was small, he was not averse to performing clerical work. He would frequently stay down at night addressing envelopes. He always insisted that all this advertising matter should be mailed at night; he gained just that much time on his competitors. On one occasion, after the force had worked well past midnight, the supply of stamps suddenly gave out. Hyde jumped into a cab, routed the postmaster out of bed, compelled him to re-open the post-office, and got his letters in before day-break.

Hyde showed this unflagging enthusiasm until the end. On the subject of the Equitable he seemed, at times, almost insane. He worked the first twenty years without a vacation, and then, broken in health, toured the world. When he gazed at the Pyramids he de-clared he saw nothing but the new Equitable build-ing; the Taj-Mahal did not compare, in his estimation, with the architecture of 120 Broadway. Ocean voyages were irksome because they destroyed his communica-tions with the home office. His worst enemies never gainsaid his devotion to the Equitable. Midnight strollers on Broadway, even in the late years, frequently noticed a few solitary lighted windows on the third floor of the Equitable Building, and little dreamed the real meaning—that the president of the society, hours after his clerks and office-boys had gone home, kept continuously at work. At certain seasons of the year he slept in the Equitable Building almost as frequently as at home. On Fortieth Street, at an early date, he purchased two adjoining houses; one he used for his home, the other he converted into an Equitable office. Once John R. Hegeman, president of the Metropolitan, hearing that Hyde was ill, called to express his sympathy; he found him surrounded by the doctors and nurses—and a stenographer on each side of his bed. He seldom made a railway journey unaccompanied by a clerical force; his breakfasts and lunches were constantly interspersed with dictation.

Hyde from the first became the Equitable's unquestioned despot. He suffered no rival near the throne. He inspired awe and trembling among the entire staff and kept the office in a constant uproar. His nervous system apparently interpenetrated the whole Equitable system. In energy, in enthusiasm, all were miniature Hydes. His very appearance largely explains the infection. He was a giant in frame and stature. His head made him a curiosity to the medical profession. He wore an eight-and-a-half hat! Occasionally his trustees, many of them the leaders in metropolitan finance, distrusted and would question his plans. Many the time he has stalked into his Board room with practically every member of his Finance Committee against him. At the sight of that huge frame and that searching eye, however, their opposition immediately melted away. He never hesitated, on occasion, openly to defy them. " I would have you all to understand," he once informed a rebellious Board, " that any director who does not agree with my ideas has the privilege of resigning! " " You don't seem to realise," he once howled at a protesting trustee, stuffing his hands in his pockets and rising on his toes, " that you are talking to Henry B. Hyde!" He had a voice that penetrated the utmost recesses of the Equitable Building. He would frequently bellow his orders fifty or a hundred feet away from the person addressed. He was subject to fits of the most violent temper, and at times would fall upon a vice-president as quickly as an office-boy. He would rake James W. Alexander fore and aft, and scold Jordan, McIntyre, and his other leading lights in the presence of strangers. Like most men of a harsh temper, he also had a vein of tenderness in his nature. He would take a sick clerk to his beautiful home at Bay Shore, Long Island, and there nurse him back to health.

He had the utmost pride and ambition for his family. He aspired to found a dynasty, and regarded the Equitable merely as a stepping-stone to this end. Early he began to pick up small blocks of stock. Hyde paid what his friends regarded as absurd prices for it. It netted only seven per cent. as an investment; but Hyde early saw and utilised the unlimited possibilities its ownership gave in controlling the society. He proposed to make this ownership an appendage to the Hyde family. His earliest hopes all settled in his oldest boy, Henry Baldwin, Jr. The finest side of his nature is brought out in his associations with this invalid child. He called him "Caleb," and made him his constant companion. In the child's last illness—he died, in his tenth year, of heart failure—Hyde would suffer no one to nurse him except himself, and even insisted on cooking all the little patient's food. Hyde's associates always declared that he was never the same man after the boy's death. As far as possible he transferred his affections and ambitions to his younger son, James Hazen. He even transferred the pet name; after his brother's death James Hazen was always known to his father as "Caleb." Hyde coddled and petted him, constantly held before his eyes the splendour of the Equitable, and taught him to regard the property as his own. And so when the younger Hyde ascended the throne he imitated in every possible way his father. He, too, became the dictator. He, too, would bawl his orders to his trembling satraps, and at the slightest sign of revolt fly into paroxysms of weak rage. He treated James W. Alexander as a cumbersome inevitability. Mr. Alexander was the President; young Hyde proceeded to show who was Boss. Alexander issued orders; young Hyde countermanded them. Thus soon two Equitable factions arose. Herein again young Hyde manifested his inferiority to his father. As long as Henry B. Hyde lived there was only one leader, one party, in the society.

How completely Hyde identified his family with the Equitable is shown by the fact that he erected a beautiful memorial window in the Equitable Building to his oldest son. In the Directors' room the most conspicuous paintings are those of himself and his father, Henry Hazen. The latter had only an incidental connection with the Equitable. He gave all his time to the Mutual Life, and died, in 1873, as its general agent in Boston. A less conspicuous picture is that of William C. Alexander, the Equitable's first president. In other more sordid ways, as we shall see, did Hyde thus identify his family with the society.

HYDE'S " EXTRA COMPENSATION "

Only such a man could have constructed one of the world's largest life-insurance companies out of nothing. From the first, however, Hyde met with unprecedented success. He wrote $100,000 the first day; by Christmas of 1859 he had scored his first million. He steadily increased his business, even during the hard times of the Civil War, and at its close had $27,000,000 to his credit. He had already demonstrated the success of his idea; had developed the modern type of life-insurance agent; had already passed by the sleepy Massachusetts companies; and was rapidly gaining on the Mutual Life. All this progress, of course, Hyde made at the expense of his policy-holders. Instead of piling up a surplus to pay "dividends," he drew upon it for agents' commissions on new business. In 1862 Hyde spent twenty-seven cents out of every dollar received, in expenses. The Equitable's charter required the distribution of surplus once in every five years. In this Hyde merely followed the established English practice.

On January 1, 1865, therefore, he was called upon to pay his first "dividends." Much mystery exists concerning that distribution. In all probability Hyde did not have much surplus available for this purpose. In the New York State report for 1865, however, the Equitable reports a "dividend" distribution of $10,-786.91, although lately it has put it at a much higher figure. Hyde paid another dividend that year, but made no official report of it. He allotted to himself, out of the surplus, $16,199.83. Those were the days of small things, but from the very first Hyde thus apparently safeguarded his own fortunes.

Hyde's salary in those years ranged from $1500 to $5000; this extra sum was a pure gratuity. So far as can be learned, Hyde had absolutely no warrant to it. When the secret got out, some ten years afterward, and Hyde, at the insurance investigation of 1877, was asked for an explanation, he declared that he had made a contract by which he was to receive two and one-half per cent. of the surplus every year, in addition to his salary. When asked if the contract was a written one, he was forced to admit that it was not. " It was simply a verbal understanding," he finally declared. Hyde was the only officer who enjoyed this bonus. Its payment entirely wiped out the Equitable's surplus. " I may say truly," Hyde remarked afterward, " that we divided among our policy-holders " (and the vice-president he did not add) " nearly all the surplus which had accumulated during the previous five years. We thus drained our coffers." The same year, as for many years afterward, the Insurance Report contains this statement: " The Equitable is purely mutual; all profits must be divided among the policy-holders." Hyde not only kept this annual percentage a secret, but deceived the insurance department concerning it. In 1867, for example, the Insurance Department propounded to the Equitable this question: "Do any of the officers of the company receive a commission or percentage on any of the business of the Company, or retiring allowances, annuities, or any other remuneration besides a fixed and regular salary?" The query could not have been more specific. The Equitable replied: "No commisions paid to officers; they receive a specific sum, as per order of the Board of Directors at their regular meeting." That very year Hyde got a secret commission of $20,060.21.[2]

A $4,000,000 EQUITABLE BUILDING

In 1865 Hyde instituted the first great reform. He conceived the idea of investing the Equitable's assets in a striking structure which should house his own company, and outwardly demonstrate to the world its greatness and financial stability. In other words, he discovered the advertising advantages of the modern office building. In this proposal Hyde again revealed that audacity which was the most striking part of his character. At that time the Equitable had only $1,500,-000 of assets; the building then projected ultimately cost $4,000,000. Hyde proposed, in other words, not only to invest all his policy-holders' reserves in a most hazardous undertaking—but he had in his treasury

[2] Insurance Investigation of 1877.

only a fraction of its cost. He confidently depended upon his own energy to get the money when the bills came in. And he did. He began work on the first Equitable Building in 1867; he did not finish it until 1876. He constructed it upon a scale of extravagance that shocked and astounded the public, and gave rise to endless scandals. In response to frequent declarations that Hyde and others made money out of this building enterprise—as well as other criticism of management—the insurance superintendent, in 1877, made a special investigation. John A. McCall, then examiner in the Department, prepared the report. He said that he had carefully examined all expenditures, all purchases of material and labour accounts, and that while these " were large, they were in accordance with law." The money expended indicates either dishonesty or the most reckless waste. This first Equitable structure was only the wing of the present building. It had a Broadway frontage of eighty-seven feet, a depth of two hundred and twenty, an extension on the rear to Pine Street, and was eight stories high. The building itself, exclusive of the land, cost $3,200,000.[8] In the early seventies construction work in New York cost just

[8] The total cost (see Insurance Investigation of 1877) was $4,000,000. Of this $700,000 or $800,000 is given as the cost of the land.

about half as much as now. The new Trinity Building, a twenty-one story marble sky-scraper, several times as large as Hyde's first Equitable office, and much more elaborately decorated, was recently put up at a total expenditure of $2,500,000. Commonplace and dingy as the first Equitable Building appears to-day, it was the architectural wonder of the age. It was as well known throughout the United States as is the Flatiron Building now. It brought the Equitable much notoriety and much advertisement; and also much reproach. " Hyde's folly " the irreverent christened it. This Equitable structure never paid. All Hyde's spare time for the next ten years was spent in fruitless efforts to justify it. It pointed the way for other companies to extravagance and waste. The Equitable and other companies have invested millions in these buildings, in the United States and Europe—almost always at a loss. This policy has been an especially aggravated source of leakage. At the present moment, for example, the Equitable maintains fifteen large office structures. Up to June, 1906, it carried nine of these at a valuation of $26,000,000. All these, on that basis, earned less than three per cent.[4] In order to maintain solvency, the Equitable must earn three and three and a half on its

[4] Superintendent Hendricks report on the Equitable assets; Page 4.

assets. Superintendent Hendricks has recently marked off $5,000,000 from this real estate—that $5,000,000 just so much money lost to the insured.

MUTUAL-EQUITABLE WAR

All these evidences of energy alarmed the Mutual Life. Frederick S. Winston at last appreciated Hyde's ability. He now saw that he had let the ablest life-insurance man of his generation slip between his fingers. In seeking some way of checking the upstart, Winston finally hit upon the plan of paying annual cash dividends. In Massachusetts Elizur Wright had preached this system for several years; and public opinion demanded its extension. Herein Winston had Hyde at a distinct disadvantage. He had heaped up a goodly surplus from forfeited policies and thus had a large fund from which to pay dividends. Hyde, after paying his 1865 " dividend," had practically no surplus at all. Moreover, as he was spending money so lavishly in his hunt for new business, he could not hope to pay satisfactory "dividends" for some years. In 1866, therefore, the Mutual, with a great flourish, announced that thereafter it would distribute its surplus annually. Hyde was equal to the emergency. He promptly declared that the Equitable would also pay annual " dividends." He was deterred not at all by the fact that he had no money in his treasury with which to pay them.

Moreover, there was another stumbling-block; his charter stipulated the division of surplus once in every five years, and thus impliedly prohibited the annual system. Hyde, however, proceeded to pay "dividends" out of an empty treasury and to violate his own charter in doing it. In the annual "dividend" competition that ensued Hyde came off badly. He could not meet the Mutual's showing. The public regularly compared his "dividends" with the Mutual's and, as a result, more largely insured in the latter company. His own policy-holders became dissatisfied with his comparatively unfavourable record. Unquestionably, in these years, Hyde paid out "dividends" which he had never realised. In fact, this is a habit which he never outgrew. Recently Joel G. Van Cise, the Equitable's actuary, testified that Hyde attempted to compel him to calculate dividends which had not been earned. Hyde's annual "dividend" system, if not a boon to his policy-holders, was at least one to himself, for he now got his percentage every year, instead of waiting quinquennial periods. In 1867 he paid himself a dividend of $20,060.21; in 1868 of $28,000; and, in 1869, of $28,-000. By this time, too, his regular salary had been raised to $7500; so that, for a small company less than ten years old, Hyde was doing fairly well. By this time, also, two others participated in the percentage combine. Thus James W. Alexander, who had become secretary in 1867, now received one-half of one per cent. of each year's surplus. George W. Philips, the actuary, got the same.

The early seventies was the period of distress among the New York life-insurance companies. If we carefully study the causes that brought so many to destruction—the Globe, the Guardian, the Continental, and the rest—we shall place the chief responsibility upon the methods pursued by the Equitable. Dishonesty in management somewhat explains the failures; but, above all, competition, reckless commissions to agents, enormous advertising expenses—on these rocks the larger number went down. At one time the New York Life, under the management of Pliny Freeman, was found insolvent;[5] and unquestionably, in the latter

[5] Testimony of Theodore M. Banta, formerly actuary and now cashier of the New York Life-Insurance Company, before the Trustees in 1887 (Beers' investigation, page 349, manuscript copy). Banta, valuing on a four per cent. basis, found a deficit in the reserves, and made the company solvent only by valuing at five per cent. It must not be assumed from this that the solvency of any of these companies is endangered now. In the sixties they did not have the enormous flexible surpluses which so amply protect them at present. Hyde's genius, as will appear, consisted in his discovery of a method that permitted all kinds of extravagance without endangering his company's solvency.

sixties, Hyde's reckless purchase of new business had
endangered the Equitable's position. Old insurance
men will tell you that, in 1868, the Equitable was practically insolvent. We can gather no intelligible idea concerning its financial condition from its reports. According to the Massachusetts standard it had, in 1868,
a surplus of only $258,000; but, in order to make even
this small showing, it included more than $700,000 of
deferred and uncollected premiums. It is hardly worth
while now to analyse the figures in detail. All companies at the time fixed up their statements practically
as they pleased, and frequently made a pretence of
solvency only by including assets that would now be
generally excluded. Real estate valuations are an extremely flexible asset, then as now; only the other day
Superintendent Hendricks reduced the Equitable's
sworn statement by $15,000,000. These facts are
clear: Hyde had been most lavish in his expenditures
for new business; had appropriated outrageous gra-
tuities for himself and inside friends; had strained his
resources by paying out dividends which he had never
earned, and thus found himself in a position that demanded immediate and drastic action. Had he been a
conservative manager, he would have cut commission
rates, and curbed extravagance in other lines. But that
would have stopped the growth of his company; above

all, interfered with his great ambition—the humiliation of the Mutual Life. He would thus have made a better showing for his insured; but that was never his first consideration. However, he could not go on indefinitely as he had started. The occasion called for a plan that would permit these enormous management expenses without alienating the public and without swamping his company.

How Hyde, in order to meet this situation and increase his own annual income, degraded the whole life-insurance system, reversed the very life-insurance idea, made the Equitable one of the world's greatest gambling institutions, and largely induced the present demoralisation, will be described in the next chapter.

CHAPTER IV

THE GREAT TONTINE GAMBLE

ONE of the most conspicuous hangers-on of the early court of Louis XIV was a certain Lorenzo Tonti, a Neapolitan banker. Tonti was one of that numerous brood of speculators who found so fruitful a field for exploitation in the European courts of the seventeenth century. Of an adventurous disposition, unlimited personal resource, and unbounded confidence in himself and his scheme, he readily wormed his way into the royal favour, became a confidential secretary to Cardinal Mazarin, a pensioner of the crown and a valued adviser on all financial affairs. He abounded in ingenious devices for increasing the national revenue, paying off the debts of the clergy, erecting great public works, and building up the foreign trade, especially in the East Indies and the South Seas. At one time he aroused much speculative interest in a plan for stimulating the growth of silk worms, by planting mulberry trees on all the highways of France. His fame rests almost entirely upon the fact, however, that he was the inventor of that scheme of gambling on human lives now generally known as Tontine.

Tonti first proposed this plan to Mazarin in 1656. Like Mazarin, however, he was an Italian, and therefore personally unpopular. Parliament refused to register the undertaking; and the public, in a spirit of ridicule, gave it its present nickname of Tontine. Tonti himself soon forfeited the royal patronage, lost his pension, and, for some reason now unknown, landed as a prisoner in the Bastile. Thence he indited many appealing letters to the King and Colbert, describing his misery and poverty and continually harping upon the advantages of Tontine. Tonti's death, which took place toward the end of the seventeenth century, is another of the many mysteries enveloping the Bastile. One of his sons was that Chevalier Tonti whose adventures among the Indians of the Northwest with La Salle and Iberville is one of the romances of early American history.

King Louis, although he neglected poor Tonti himself, never entirely abandoned his scheme. In 1689, when surrounded by a European coalition, harassed for money and unable to borrow further from the bankers or to wring another penny in taxes from his exhausted peasantry, he raised 1,400,000 livres on the Tontine plan. He followed precisely the programme mapped

out by Tonti more than thirty years before. He invited
subscriptions, at 300 livres each, to a general fund.
He agreed to pay the total interest on this fund to all
surviving subscribers. Each member's share of the income was to cease at death and revert to those who
still lived. Each member's income, that is, increased
in proportion to the deaths of his associates. It was
clearly a lottery in annuities, in which the prizes went
to the long-lived members. It acquired popularity because of this gambling feature, and because it apparently promised a provision for old age. Its essential
advantage to the King was that the capital fund itself
need never be redeemed. It was a state loan, that is,
upon which interest only was paid, and which was entirely liquidated when the final survivor died.

King Louis' first Tontine apparently had a successful career. It met all its obligations fairly and continued until 1726. The solitary survivor was a widow,
one Charlotte Barbier, who died in her ninety-sixth
year. At that time she drew an annual income of 73,000
livres, in return for an original subscription of 300.
King Louis and his successors frequently utilised this
method of supplementing the public funds. In the
eighteenth century private speculators also established
a large number of Tontines; in France there was little
less than a Tontine craze. Nearly all these private un-

dertakings, however, ended disastrously. In most instances the Tontine managers were dishonest. The greatest private Tontine, the Caisse La Farge, cheated the public out of nearly 60,000,000 francs. Dishonesty was inherent in the plan itself. Tonti did not devise his original scheme in the interest of the people, but of the government. " I believe this is an easy way," he wrote to Colbert from the Bastile, " whereby the King may get several millions from his people which would never be subject to redemption. The King might use them to redeem his domain, and for the execution of other designs. This might be done without its being known. It transforms France into a gold mine for the monarchy." Private capitalists adopted the plan in an identical spirit: to get a large capital fund which they might use for their own immediate purposes, and which they never need pay back. Their swindlings became so outrageous that ultimately the state prohibited Tontines by law. In England and America the idea was chiefly utilised as a method of raising money for public buildings and hotels. In this case the property was held intact and ultimately divided among certain nominated survivors. The Tontine Coffee House, in New York, at Wall and Pearl Streets, was financed on this basis. These enterprises also usually failed of complete success. Toward the close of the eighteenth century there was no more odious word in Europe than Tontine.

HYDE ADDS THE TONTINE SYSTEM OF LIFE INSURANCE

About 1868 some ingenious person directed Henry B. Hyde's attention to the career of this same Lorenzo Tonti. We might not inappropriately compare the Equitable Society in 1868 with the French government in 1689; and Hyde's financial position with that of Louis XIV. Like the French king, Hyde had outlined a long and expensive campaign of conquest. He sought to humble all his competitors, to give the Equitable the leadership among American life-insurance companies. Like Louis, too, he had deeply invaded his treasury by bitterly contested wars and needed money supplies for their further prosecution. Hyde was thus in a mood to adopt almost any new insurance scheme, especially when, in addition to these purposes, it seemed likely to increase his own annual income.

In 1868, therefore, the Equitable announced, with much expensive advertising, a new "discovery in life insurance." It flooded the country with circulars duly setting forth the "greatest reform thus far promulgated by any life-insurance company." Up to that time the Equitable had dealt only in straight, conventional life insurance. It had issued only life endow-

ment, and term policies. Now, however, it radically
changed its programme, and began to handle an entirely
novel brand. It offered a new form of policy, and
named it Tontine, in honour of the Italian adventurer
whose theories it embodied. This policy combined two
distinct principles: the payment of a definite sum in
the event of death, and the chance at a money prize
in case the insured survived a stipulated period. The
insurance indemnity was, of course, a fixed sum—the
face of the policy; the amount to be won by the survivors, however, was indefinite, or depended upon several contingencies. Hyde did not call this ultimate
payment to survivors, however, a " prize "; he called
it an " investment return."

In order to add a Tontine attraction to the regulation life-insurance policy, Hyde necessarily had to
make important modifications. According to the original French idea you subscribed a stipulated amount
and reaped incommensurate rewards if you outlived
your associates. Your income began coincidentally
with your entrance into the pool; its increase only depended upon continued survivorship. Hyde, however,
proposed to adopt arbitrarily a certain period during
which the Tontine fund should accumulate. Each year
he grouped the Tontine policy-holders in three separate classes—those who elected to remain in the pool

ten, fifteen, and twenty years. In 1870, for example, Hyde may have had 15,000 Tontine policy-holders. Of these perhaps 5000 entered the ten-year class. The group would have a separate Tontine fund, which would be divided among all who were alive in 1880, and had kept up their premium payments. Another 5000 may have adopted the fifteen-year class. For them also would be accumulated another Tontine fund, divisible among the survivors in 1885. The last 5000 may have chosen the twenty-year class. These would divide up their Tontine prizes in 1890. Meanwhile, if any member in good standing—if he had regularly paid his premiums, in other words—died at any time, his family received the amount for which he had insured; if he lived until his period expired, he got his share of the Tontine winnings; if he failed to pay the premiums, he got nothing at all. Ostensibly the purpose of arranging ten, fifteen, and twenty year classes was to accommodate the periods to the ages of the insured. A young man might reasonably enter the twenty-year class, because of his natural hopes of survival; an old man the ten or fifteen, because his chances of survival were not so promising.

Herein, therefore, we have three separate classes each year. In reality Hyde proposed an even more bewildering number of groupings. He added his Tontine feature to all kinds of policies: endowments, ten payments, fifteen payments, and so on. Had he actually maintained his programme, he might have had in the neighbourhood of 200 classifications in a number of years. In practice, however, Hyde ignored these distributions. All Tontine policy-holders on all plans he grouped together, and distributed the winnings among them practically as he pleased.

TONTINE FUND HEAPED UP FROM FORFEITURES

The essential feature of the plan was the abandonment of the annual dividend system which the Equitable had adopted in 1866. Tontine policy-holders, instead of receiving back the excess cost of their insurance every year, agreed to forego it for ten, fifteen, or twenty years, according to the particular class they elected to enter. Under the original Tontine plan there were two great sources of accretion to the Tontine surplus: the amounts usually paid as " surrender values " to retiring members, and the amounts popularly known as " dividends." In other words, Hyde fed the Tontine fund from the two great life-insurance accumulations: " reserve " and " surplus." The reserve has already been described as the deduction made from the premiums paid in the early years to cover the increased insurance cost of the later. It is the inevitable consequence of the modern level premium system, the only one which has thus far proved practically successful. In order that one may pay the same sum every year and not one annually increasing, the actuaries " average the matter up." At age forty, the usual net price charged per $1000 for straight life insurance is $23. Its actual cost at that age is about $9. The difference, $14, is the amount you contribute to the insurance expense of those later years when the actual cost exceeds the premium charged. This excess is called the " reserve." If you drop the policy you are thus in this position: You have paid the full cost of your insurance for the years it has been in force, and have contributed a reserve which, in part, is to meet the expense of later years. If you drop your policy, obviously justice demands that you take this reserve cost with you. If it is not paid back, clearly you have contributed money for which you have received no insurance equivalent. Inasmuch as a mutual company ostensibly seeks to furnish insurance at its actual cost and give value received for every penny paid in, surrender values are an essential part of its structure.

Up to 1861 most companies ignored this simple principle. For generations this fact has been the standing reproach of life insurance. In England, especially in the first half of the nineteenth century, the managers of life companies had waxed fat and wealthy by forfeiting the reserves of their retiring members. In America, thanks to the sleepless work of Elizur Wright, their claims had for the first time received general recognition. He had secured the passage of the first non-forfeiture law in 1861, and had gradually educated policy-holders to demand, in case of withdrawal, a certain percentage of what they had paid in. The Massachusetts companies, because of the non-forfeiture features of their policies, became widely popular. New York State had passed no non-forfeiture law, but competition had compelled the New York companies, including the Equitable, to adopt a modified non-forfeiture system. The lapse rate in the later sixties, however, was enormous. Of every 100 policies issued, only about ten per cent. expired by death or maturity. The rest were surrendered or lapsed for non-payment of premium. Herein Hyde found his great opportunity. He proposed to stop paying surrender values to his lapsing Tontine policy-holders, and to contribute the amounts which lapsing members would ordinarily have received to his Tontine fund.

Let us consider in some detail precisely what this meant. Below is given a table of surrender values and their equivalents in insurance now paid at various periods upon a $10,000 ordinary life policy issued at ages forty and fifty: *

In other words, if you insure at age forty for $10,-000, pay for twenty years and then drop out, you are entitled to a cash value of $3830, or a paid-up policy of $5750. If you insure under similar conditions at age fifty, and discontinue after twenty years, you take either $4980 cash or a paid-up policy for $6410. These are your mathematical equities, under contract, after the company has deducted the cost of carrying your insurance for twenty years. The payment of these equities is no more than life-insurance justice; anything else, in a mutual company, is little better than robbery.

* The figures are those paid at present by the Equitable.

Age 40

If Lapsed	Surrender value in cash	Surrender value in paid-up insurance
After 5 years	$ 670	$1490
" 10 "	1770	3190
" 15 "	2780	4560
" 20 "	3830	5750

Age 50

If Lapsed	Surrender value in cash	Surrender value in paid-up insurance
After 5 years	$ 980	$1820
" 10 "	2510	3760
" 15 "	3780	5220
" 20 "	4980	6410

FAMILY PROTECTION A STAKE IN A HUGE GAMBLE

Under the Tontine plan you forfeited, on lapse, your whole money interest in the policy. This surrender value was usually paid, not in cash, but in insurance. Thus, if forced out, you obtained, in addition to the insurance during the period the policy ran, a paid-up policy which was the insurance equivalent of your reserve accumulation. If you remained in for any considerable period, that policy, as we have seen, might represent a considerable amount. It was the only financial protection your family held against your death. Hyde now calmly proposed that you place this insurance in jeopardy; make your family protection a stake in his Tontine lottery. If you lost in this game— dropped out, that is, before the Tontine period expired —you left your wife and children absolutely unprovided for; if you won—stayed in until the end—your family received the insurance for which your own premiums had paid, and its proportion of the insurance paid for by the premiums of those who had been closed out. Manifestly the odds stood strongly in favour of the rich. Those who discontinued their payments usually did so because of poverty. The richer policy-holders, however, had no difficulty in keeping up their premiums. Obviously, therefore, Tontine was merely a plan by

which the more affluent policy-holders could appropriate the insurance of their less fortunate associates.

ALL " DIVIDENDS " DIVERTED TO THE TONTINE POOL

Hyde also heaped up his Tontine fund by generally
forfeiting " dividends." Again we must keep clearly in
mind precisely what this " dividend " is. The word, as
explained in the first chapter, is an unfortunate mis-
nomer. If it could be eliminated from the nomenclature
of life insurance, the situation would clear immensely.
Life-insurance prices are based upon two fundamental
assumptions: that a certain number of people will die
every year, and that the money laid aside as reserve
will earn a certain rate of interest. To the premium
thus ascertained the company adds a certain percentage for expenses, called the loading. If the anticipated
deaths occurred precisely as indicated; if exactly the
expected interest on reserve were earned; if the managements spent for administrative purposes and commissions the sum provided by the premium loadings—
the cost of the insurance would be identically what was
charged. Inasmuch as all these elements vary, the
actual cost of insurance varies also. In order to safe-
guard itself against fluctuations, however, the company
always charges an excess price. Thus, at the end of

every year, it finds itself in possession of a certain sum of money over and above the actual cost of that year's insurance and reserve. This excess cost is the so-called surplus; its repayment to policy-holders the "dividend." The dividend, therefore, it cannot be too frequently insisted upon, is not a dividend at all, but merely the return of an overpayment.

In Hyde's early Equitable days these "dividends" or overpayments were accumulated for five-year periods, and then returned. In the early years Hyde unquestionably largely drew upon them to pay agents' commissions, percentages, and other management expenses.

In other words, he brought in his new policy-holders at the expense of the old. He could safely do this so long as the dividend distributions were postponed for considerable periods, inasmuch as his practice would not be readily detected. But, in 1866, competition with the Mutual Life compelled him to return these overpayments every year. The small "dividends" then paid clearly showed that he had drawn upon them heavily for acquisition expenses of new business. "Mr. Hyde frequently told me," said John A. McCall, in effect, at the recent New York insurance investigation, "that he had to abandon the annual dividend system simply because he could not meet the competition of

the Mutual Life." The Equitable's great lapse rate
for the years from 1866 to 1868—its annual dividend
period—clearly reflects the existing dissatisfaction.
Manifestly the honest practice would have been a general retrenchment of expenses, and the return to all
policy-holders of their annual overpayments. That,
however, did not coincide with Hyde's ambitions. Instead, he decided to drop the annual system entirely,
and to add these dividends, or overpayments, to the
Tontine fund. If you died before your Tontine period
expired, you obtained no "dividends" at all; if you
lapsed you also forfeited them. Your "dividends," in
either of these events, went into the Tontine surplus
for division among the survivors.

Briefly, therefore, the theory of the Tontine programme may thus be summarised:

A. *If you died before the end of the Tontine period,
your beneficiaries received the face of the policy; but
no "dividends."*

B. *If you lapsed, you got no "dividends" and no
"surrender value." You lost every cent you had paid,
and the insurance which it would have purchased.*

C. *If you lived to the end of the Tontine period and
regularly paid your premiums, you got your own dividends and your share of (a) the "dividends" of those
who had died, and (b) the "dividends" and surrender*

*values, or reserves, of those who had lapsed—all accu-
mulated at compound interest.*[7]

ONLY ONE OUT OF THREE COULD WIN

In this great gamble Hyde had carefully calculated
the chances of success. He presented figures, professedly
based upon general experience, showing the expected
number of lapses and deaths. He declared—and, in fact,
recommended his new insurance on this ground—that,
of every 1000 at age thirty-seven who began the game,
and elected the twenty-year period, only 353 would
survive to divide up the profits. That is to say, only
about one man in three could possibly win. His leading
actuary apologetically said that, in all probability, not
even this many would survive; that his estimates had

[7] The Tontine policy must not be confused with an ordinary
endowment. An endowment is a perfectly legitimate, though
somewhat expensive, form of life insurance. It guarantees the
payment of a particular sum in case of death or the survival
to the end of a particular period. The amount, in both cases,
is clearly specified in the contract. A Tontine policy specifies
the amount to be paid at death; but makes no guarantee concerning the amount to be paid on survival. The Tontine feature
had absolutely no connection with life insurance; it was a special
fund, devised as described above, for division among those who
remained in the pool. It was added to endowment policies as
well as to ordinary life. Endowments also accumulate reserves
and dividends; Tontine funds were accumulated from them and
divided among the surviving endowment policy-holders, precisely
as in the case of ordinary life.

been extremely conservative, and based upon figures "less favourable" than those experienced by other companies. By "less favourable" he meant that more lapses would probably take place than he had counted upon; that is, that more families would forfeit their insurance; and that the prizes for the persistent members, consequently, would be larger.

In this lottery, moreover, you played for an indefinite stake. In other gambling games you usually know what, in case of success, you are to receive. You put ten dollars on this horse; you lay twenty on the turn of a particular card. If your horse wins, you get your ten dollars; if your card turns up, you pocket your twenty. Any other policy would be an incitement to riot. In Tontine, however, you laid down a specific sum every year; but, even though fortune went your way, you hadn't the slightest idea what the prize would be. It was a blind pool with a vengeance. Hyde guaranteed no winnings. He stipulated in every contract— every policy, that is—that, at the expiration of the Tontine period, each survivor's share "should be equitably apportioned by the company." In other words, the company—that is, Hyde himself—could give you just as much, or just as little, as it chose. If it handed over nothing at all, the policy-holder had absolutely no redress. As we shall see, many disgruntled prize winners, when their bonuses fell so far below their anticipations, appealed to the courts for a more "equitable" share. The learned judges informed them that the company had absolute jurisdiction over the distribution; that the policy-holders may have made a foolish and one-sided contract, but that they had made a contract all the same. Any gambling-house conducted "on the level" assumes direct obligations to the winners, but the Equitable did not. Hyde held the advantageous position of a stakeholder in a bet who had secretly arranged the programme so that he could himself manipulate the money in hand, and pay over to the successful gambler precisely as much or as little as he willed. Many policy-holders, finally waking up, attempted to retire. Then they discovered that Hyde had safely locked them up for anywhere from ten to twenty years. Their only revenge was to cease paying premiums. That was precisely what the Equitable above all desired; for then, everything they had paid was immediately swallowed by the Tontine pool.

ONE-HALF THE POLICY-HOLDERS DEPRIVED OF PAID-FOR INSURANCE

Hyde's Tontine scheme thus ostentatiously deprived one-half of his policy-holders of their paid-for insurance. Its success depended upon the number of widows and children it left unprovided for. The more lapses Hyde secured, the more helpless families he despoiled, the greater company the Equitable became. He accompanied his Tontine announcement with certain estimates as to possible Tontine profits. Eminent mathematicians have calculated the amount of suffering which he thus proposed. He figured, for example, that every policy-holder aged thirty who insured for $10,000 and who managed to live and keep up his premiums for twenty years, would receive a cash prize of $7120. If 10,000 men insured on that basis, precisely 6882 would have to forfeit all their insurance in order to give the re-maining 2498 [8] that additional bonus. This minority would divide up some $7,400,000 cash, forfeited by those forced out of the pool. That $7,400,000 would have provided at least $17,000,000 of paid-up insur-ance. As the amount of the average policy was about $2000, that would have provided insurance protection for 8500 helpless families. For the last few years the Equitable has written in the neighbourhood of $300,-000,000 of insurance in a year. To realise the expected Tontine profits on that amount, Hyde would have con-fiscated at least $57,000,000 of paid-for insurance— or, on the basis given above, the insurance protection of 28,500 families. Precisely what was the lapse rate on Tontine policies we probably shall never know. On

[8] 620 would die.

this subject, Henry B. Hyde was questioned at length at the New York Insurance Investigation of 1877. Did he know the number of Tontine policies which had been forfeited in 1876? No, sir, he did not. Did he know the number and amount of Tontine policies which had been forfeited since the system began? No, sir, he did not. Had he any intention of making public these facts? No, sir, he had not. In 1885 the New York and Ohio legislatures appointed committees to discover this and other facts concerning Tontine, but without result. The lapse rate, however, must have been enormous. From 1870, when the Tontine scheme began, until 1885, when the issuing of full Tontine policies ceased, the Equitable wrote $613,000,000 of new insurance; in the same period it lapsed $400,000,000—or 65 per cent. of the whole. Probably at least two-thirds of this was Tontine.

THE TONTINE FUND DRAWN UPON FOR AGENTS' COMMISSIONS

What was Hyde's purpose in thus disregarding the very purpose of life insurance itself? In the first place, as we have seen, he wished to escape comparisons, as to dividends earned, with other companies. By postponing them for long periods he cleverly concealed the real situation; and meanwhile talked loudly as to what

they would be, when those periods expired. Again, he
needed a large surplus upon which he could draw for
management expenses, especially in his war with the
Mutual Life. Hyde, as has been proved, neatly escaped
all responsibility for these Tontine dividends. Thus he
had a huge reserve war chest, which he could draw
upon as occasion required. He could use it in paying
excessive agents' commissions, salaries, bonuses, and
prizes; in reckless advertising and in other expensive
methods of insurance propagandism. In other words,
that he might build up a great institution and kill off
his competitors, he proposed to pay part of his policy-
holders' dividends and the surrender values of lapsing
members to his faithful agents. He made this surplus
serve other purposes. He found it extremely useful
as an advertisement. As its size increased year by
year, he pointed to it as a sign of impregnable financial strength. He compared it with the smaller surpluses
heaped up by annual dividend companies, omitting all
reference, of course, to the salient point—that he had a
large surplus because he withheld his dividends; and that
his rivals had proportionately small ones because they
distributed them every year. He found his campaign
cry, " Surplus is Strength," an eloquent enticement to
new business. Here once more he contradicted himself.
On the one hand he declared again and again that his

surplus all belonged to present policy-holders and could not be used for other purposes. On the other he sedulously cultivated the idea that the surplus, in case of necessity, could be drawn upon to strengthen the Equitable's reserves. Again, he made new policy-holders believe that here was a huge dividend fund in which they might participate; while, according to his original theory, the surplus represented accumulations on the funds of old policy-holders, among whom it must be eventually divided.

A SOURCE OF PRIVATE GAIN TO HYDE

From the very first, the surplus proved a source of personal gain. The Tontine system automatically increased the annual compensation of the Equitable's chief executive officers. In addition to his salary, Hyde received $2\frac{1}{2}$ per cent. of the surplus every year.[9] James W. Alexander, at the same time, received one-half of one per cent.; and George W. Phillips, the actuary, the same amount. Manifestly, the larger the surplus, the larger this annual percentage. If Hyde distributed

[9] Testimony of Henry B. Hyde at the Insurance Investigation of 1877. Page 88 (Manning's edition).

Q. That was on the basis of $2\frac{1}{2}$ per cent. of the surplus? A. Yes, sir.

Q. In the hands of the company at the end of each year? A. Yes, sir.

this surplus annually, however, his profits would never be abnormally large, because the surplus itself would be comparatively small. But if he accumulated it for twenty years, what limitless possibilities of gain! Hyde proposed for all his policy-holders a ten, fifteen, or twenty year division; but intended, as usual, to take his own percentage every year. He wished to place his insured upon the deferred dividend basis; but the annual system was still good enough for him. Observe how this Tontine system increased his annual earnings. Under the annual system, for example, you received, perhaps, a first year's dividend cf $100. Hyde would get $2\frac{1}{2}$ per cent. of that, or $2.50. That ended his participation. But if you took a twenty year Tontine, that $100 remained in the pool for twenty years, and Hyde got his $2.50 every year. In the second year you received a dividend of $125. Under the annual system Hyde could get just a single percentage, or $3.12. But under the Tontine scheme he would get that $3.12 for nineteen years. Thus every year Hyde, Alexander, and Phillips appropriated together $3\frac{1}{2}$ per cent. of the surplus. As the Equitable earned only a little more than 5, this left only about $1\frac{1}{2}$ per cent. of the interest increase for the insured. And yet one of the chief sources of Tontine winnings, according to Hyde's representations, were the "wonderful results accomplished by compound interest." In fact, Tontine did very largely increase Hyde's annual income. His "extra compensation" jumped, under the Tontine stimulus, from $6000 to $50,000 per annum. Its ultimate discovery, and the great scandal caused thereby, led to its abandonment. Actually, however, Hyde never gave it up; it was ostensibly in exchange for this "surrendered contract"—which, as we have seen, was never a contract, but a "verbal understanding"—that his wife received, after his death, her $25,000 pension. This "contract," if in force now, would entitle the President of the Equitable to $1,000,000 a year. Thus may be traced the genesis of the deferred dividend system to a percentage on the surplus secretly enjoyed by Henry B. Hyde. Hyde personally profited by the surplus in other ways, as will duly appear; but, at the very beginning, it was thus immediately identified with his private fortunes.

WHY THE TONTINE SURPLUS WAS MADE AN ASSET

Others have detected, in the Tontine scheme, an even more far-reaching plan. They have declared that Hyde aimed at heaping up a huge surplus, the ownership of which would ultimately vest in the holders of Equitable stock, that is, in Hyde himself.

This interpretation is apparently supported by the fact that the Equitable for many years has carried its Tontine surplus not as a liability, which, of course, it is, but as an asset. The present writer does not believe that this was Hyde's original idea. Temperamentally he was incapable of any such far-reaching plan. He lived entirely in the present, and never mapped out a programme more than a year ahead. He was essentially an opportunist. He adopted Tontine—to sum up the situation—to save the Equitable from threatened bankruptcy, to avoid unfavourable comparisons with other companies, to obtain a large fund for expenses, to get a basis for glittering promises of profits and thus entice new business; and also, unquestionably, to increase his own annual income. These were the immediate necessities of the moment; beyond that, Hyde seldom gave a thought. Afterward the Equitable management also found it a convenient protection against their own dishonesty. Had it not been for the Tontine surplus the Equitable unquestionably would have gone to the scrap-heap years ago. Scores of other companies which imitated Hyde's agency methods failed in the '70's; had they adopted Tontine they probably would have weathered the storm. Some strangely perverted casuists advance this as an argument in favour of Tontine. But these companies became embarrassed because of wild extravagance and dishonesty; and went down because they could not recoup with the forfeited dividends of their insured. The Equitable's management also became extravagant and dishonest, but Hyde made good the hiatus with the Tontine accumulations. Manifestly the cure really demanded was not Tontine, but the reform of the original abuses. Hyde made this surplus an asset, in order to save the Equitable from insolvency.

This change was made in 1877. That was a terrible year in life-insurance history. Almost every month some company collapsed. The Equitable's policy-holders lived in daily dread. The society was investigated three times in as many months; once by the insurance committee of the New York Senate, once by its own policy-holders, and once by the insurance department. " I can't transact any business," said Hyde, " I spend all my time being investigated." John A. McCall, then deputy superintendent, made the official examination. The Equitable's liabilities, according to the rigid Massachusetts standard, were $29,425,650. Its assets were $30,872,374. Included in the latter were the New York and Boston buildings, grossly overvalued at more than $5,000,000, and the stock of the Mercantile Trust Company at $1,525,405. The value of that stock at that time was problematical; a year or two before the Mercantile Trust Company had been on the brink of insolvency itself. Even accepting the New York liberal standard of valuation, which placed the liabilities at $26,231,141, the showing was not at all favourable. In order to make the society solvent beyond dispute, Mr. McCall quietly transferred the Tontine surplus, then amounting to $2,193,-577, from the column of liabilities to that of assets. It has remained there ever since.

Hyde found several obstacles in the way of his reform. His own charter, as we have seen, required the distribution of surplus once in every five years. Hyde succeeded in getting through a law which changed all that. No one at the time suspected his purpose; his law seemed the perfection of innocence. It was entitled: " A law authorising the payment of annual dividends." It was thus a sneak bill; it provided that any life-insurance corporation " which, by its charter, or articles of association, is restricted to making a dividend only once in two or more years, may hereafter, notwithstanding anything to the contrary in such charter or articles, make and pay over dividends annually, *or at longer intervals*," etc. Thus Hyde, in a law which on its face authorised annual dividends, interjected a clause which apparently permitted him to declare them at such intervals as he chose—and, for that matter,

not at all. The influences back of this measure are
obscure. The insurance papers of the day make not
the slightest comment on it; the insurance report of
1869 has only a perfunctory reference. No insurance
law, however, has had more far-reaching and unfortunate consequences; it has been appealed to for years
as the legal support of the deferred dividend system.
Eminent authorities, however, have always questioned
whether it actually authorised Tontine; many still
maintain that the Equitable and other New York companies, in deferring dividends, have persistently violated their own charters.

Hyde's first Tontine plan, proposed in 1868, was
a little too complicated, and the public did not readily
favour it. Not until 1871 did he begin to make great
headway. In that year he recast and rechristened it.
He announced, with a great flourish of trumpets, his
celebrated " Tontine Savings Fund Policy." His pam-
phlet for that year is one of the curiosities of life-
insurance literature. In this Hyde boldly announced
his abandonment of all conservative life-insurance principles. " It will be seen," he said, " that the Tontine
principle is precisely the reverse of that upon which
Life Assurance is based. In the former case the motive
is essentially selfish; in the latter, it is the result of
one of the noblest and most unselfish aspirations which

can animate the human breast—the desire for securing
a provision for those who are dependent upon our ex-
ertions for support when death shall have called us
away." And yet Hyde now proclaimed his abandonment of this high ideal; and his adoption of the system
which was " essentially selfish " and the " reverse " of
" the principles upon which Life Assurance was based."
His arguments were ingeniously specious. Under his
Tontine plan, he declared, the great end of life insurance was achieved; that is, in case of death, the actual
face value of the policy was paid. He simply proposed
to withhold from those who died early all dividends,
and to pay them, together with the accumulations from
lapses, to those who survived the Tontine period. Thus,
said Hyde, he equalised the burdens of life insurance.
The injustice of the old system rested upon the fact
that those who died early paid very small amounts for
the benefits their families received; while those who
lived long frequently paid in more than the face of
the policies. By withholding all surplus from the
former and paying it to the latter he thus secured a
fine balance of justice. Hyde knew, of course, the fal-
lacy and absurdity of this argument. As has previ-
ously been explained, no one ever cheats a life-insurance company; whether he dies ten minutes after obtaining his policy, or fifty years afterward, he pays

the company precisely what it costs to carry his insurance. In making up its rates the company figures upon so many deaths the first year, so many the second, and so on. It makes no difference whether *you* die that first year, or *I;* the company has simply realised the death it had prepared for and upon which it has based its charges. Hyde, however, saw the great popular value of this argument; it met the vulgar objection to life insurance that "you had to die to win." Hyde had more difficulty in excusing the greatest iniquity of his system: his wholesale confiscation of the reserves of lapsing members. By stigmatising these as "deserters," as renegades, who, having abandoned their policies, had no claim upon the company's consideration, he even blinded the public on this score. These deserters, however, as has already been said, formed more than 90 per cent. of all policy-holders of the time, and were the unfortunate classes who were usually forced by unexpected poverty to cease their payments.

"EXPERT" ENDORSEMENTS OF TONTINE

Hyde gathered to his support the most influential people in society and finance. He widely advertised the endorsement of twenty-one of the leading merchants and bankers of New York City. He also backed up

Tontine by much actuarial authority. He had annexed
Sheppard Homans to the Equitable after the latter's
quarrel with the Mutual Life. Homans' reputation
stood high; next to Elizur Wright, he was probably
the foremost American authority. Homans had much
to do with formulating the original scheme, and from
the first remained its warmest sponsor. The New York
Life, which immediately followed the Equitable, re-
tained Elizur Wright as a possible defender. Wright
gave a characteristic opinion. He endorsed the mathematical accuracy of the computations, but followed
this with a whole-souled condemnation of the plan.
The New York Life never published this " endorsement." In public Wright denounced Tontine as " life-
insurance cannibalism." " Its sole and only function,"
he added, " is to make the richer part of the company
richer by making the poorer part poorer. It is as if
a temperance society should endeavour to promote its
cause by establishing a liquor saloon under its lecture-
room, or a church should support its minister by a
lottery." Others, however, Hyde found more amen-
able. He early enlisted the support of William Barnes,
the New York Superintendent of Insurance. " The Tontine system," said Mr. Barnes, in a letter which Equitable agents extensively used in soliciting Tontine business, " seems so natural and applicable to certain classes

of policy-holders, that like many important discoveries in science and art, the wonder is how it could have remained so long dormant and undiscovered. Especial credit is due to the man, or men, who conceived the thought of collecting the *Tontine tendencies* of men and applying this momentum to the development and spreading of Life Assurance." Mr. Barnes was the son-in-law of Thurlow Weed, and high in the councils of the Republican party. He is now more than eighty years old, but has never lost his interest in insurance or politics. He has lately acquired much notoriety as the defender of modern life-insurance methods, and is as strenuously the champion of the deferred dividend system as he was thirty-eight years ago.

Hyde fortified these arguments by the most extravagant estimates of what the Tontine winnings would be. He baited in thousands by making promises which he never fulfilled, and which, at the time, he must have known he never could make good. No patent medicine was ever more extravagantly advertised. Our old friend, Charlotte Barbier, the fortunate widow who under Louis XIV.'s first Tontine obtained an annual revenue of 74,000 livres in return for a subscription of 300, was pushed to the front, in Equitable literature, on all possible occasions. Men who had taken Tontines, with satisfactory results, wrote letters which were widely published as advertisements—another adaptation of a popular patent medicine device. Hyde called the Tontine policy " endowment insurance at life rates." He asserted, that is, that, for an ordinary life premium, the accumulated surplus and reserve, at the end of the period, would equal the face of the policy— that is, be the same as an endowment. He declared that this same surplus would purchase an annuity large enough to pay all future premiums and a life income besides! Under a Tontine policy, that is, you ceased paying after twenty years; but your insurance still went on, and you got an income in addition. " After the dividends arrived," said an official Equitable circular, " there would be the requirement of no more premiums, the assurant receiving, instead, a considerable annuity commencing just at the time when age begins to impair the faculties!" Hyde declared again and again that a Tontine policy was safer and more profitable than a United States gold bond. He claimed that the Tontine dividends would be *three or four* times as large as those paid on the annual plan. He especially recommended a Tontine policy to those who had mortgaged homes. Insure, he said, for the amount of the mortgage; if you die, the policy will pay it off; if you live, the dividends will not only pay the interest, but a fair size annuity.

THE " BLUE BOOKS " OF ESTIMATES

Even more mendacious were the famous " blue books " which Hyde placed in every agent's hands. He originated that practice, since become so general, of showing prospective policy-holders' written estimates of " investment " returns. Hyde's actuaries had worked the whole thing out in detail, and formulated precise figures for every age and every period and every form of policy. Hyde had sufficient shrewdness, however, never to guarantee these figures; and guardedly informed the agents that they were only " estimates." On this ground the Equitable sought to escape responsibility when the actual dividends fell so far below Hyde's glowing anticipations. That, however, has never been accepted as a satisfactory excuse. Here was a great life-insurance company; on its surface, a great trust institution, whose every word should have been honour and truth and justice; and now it placed in the hands of thousands of agents, many ignorant, many untruthful, most having in view only a single end —a commission—a book containing in detail the most extravagant promises. Was it to be expected that, competition being what it was, they should inform their clients that these figures were only " estimates "? Of course they carefully avoided this particular point.

Conservatism has never been a striking characteristic of Equitable agents; and their clients almost invariably regarded the figures furnished them as actual guarantees. They did not know that these estimates were never incorporated in the policy; that the agent's glib promises in no way legally bound the company; and that, far from receiving the promised bonuses, the Equitable had not contracted to pay them anything at all. Neither did they know that the agent had been admonished to sell nothing but Tontine policies; that he was paid extravagant commissions for doing so; and that these commissions usually exceeded these paid on old line insurance. As always, the agent was some particular friend, and was relied upon implicitly for advice as to the most desirable form of policy. In this country to-day are thousands who were taken in by this glowing propaganda of the early '70's; many are probably reading these very lines. Leading experts warned them time and time again, but unavailingly, that their expectations could never be realised. Eminent actuaries, here and in Europe, riddled the "blue books," demonstrating their bad faith. The life-insurance surplus, as already explained, is derived from three sources—excess interest on reserve, excess loadings for expense, and decreased mortality. In the old Tontine days the profits from lapses also went in. Hyde based his Tontine estimate on a six per cent. interest rate; at that time the Equitable earned something more than five—and regularly earned less in the succeeding years. Hyde figured upon the usual number of lapses, ignoring the fact that the Tontine scheme, by so heavily penalising withdrawals, would tend to keep people in. Above all, he based his great profits upon expected retrenchments in management expenses! He figured upon a 12½ per cent. expense rate; at that very time the Equitable spent 16 per cent. of its premium income and, in succeeding years, ran it up to 25. Sheppard Homans is generally credited with having prepared these estimates. In this one act he irretrievably ruined his reputation. He became, afterward, merely a hanger-on of Hyde; his widow, up to a few months ago, drew a pension from the Equitable. Homans' original estimates were much larger than those actually published, and were cut down at the suggestion of J. G. VanCise, at that time a clerk in the Equitable's actuarial department.

THREE DIFFERENT BLUE BOOKS IN ONE YEAR

That these estimates could never have been honestly made is evident from the fact that in 1886 the Equitable had three separate blue books in the agents' hands. On January 1, 1886, Hyde issued an entirely new vol-

HENRY HAZEN HYDE

ume of estimates. This made so considerable a reduction that the agents raised a great howl. As a result it was withdrawn, after having been in circulation less than a month, and the agents directed to solicit business on the estimates of 1883. In the fall. Hyde withdrew this book and issued another, giving entirely new estimates. For example, in January the Equitable informed a prospective $10,000 policy-holder, aged forty, that in twenty years his cash profit would amount to $3795.70. " We can't get business on so low an estimate as that!" shouted the agents. The Equitable, therefore, authorised the promise of a cash bonus of $7166. In October the society split the difference between these two estimates and placed the figures at $5925.70.

APPEALING TO THE " TONTINE TENDENCIES " OF MEN

We must thank William Barnes for one telling phrase, which, in itself, sufficiently explains the Equitable's success. Hyde had " collected the Tontine tendencies of men." He had appealed, that is, to their gambling instinct. Into every hamlet went his agents with their " blue books," selling not primarily family protection but possible prizes in a great insurance lottery. They always tellingly appealed to the individual man. " Take a Tontine policy," they said. " Look at the enormous returns if you survive this Tontine period. You will get not only your own profits, but part of the profits of all that die! *You* will not die; *you* are strong, in good health—*you* will be sure to live. But thousands in your class will die, and by every one of those deaths you will profit. Moreover, look at the enormous number who will lapse their policies. Do you know that nine out of every ten who purchase life insurance drop out? Under our Tontine scheme these poor devils won't get a cent; everything they have paid goes into the surplus to be divided among the survivors. Of course *you* won't drop out. *You* are well-to-do, and will have no trouble in meeting all your payments." This appeal took like wild-fire. As long as human nature retains its gambling instinct, it always will. Thousands willingly staked their own chances of living and paying against the similar chances of their fellow-insurers. They readily risked all their own life insurance for a possibility of getting a part of that of their less fortunate associates.

Thus Hyde placed in the hands of hundreds of agents his " blue books " and sent them forth to preach the gospel of Tontine. He raided the leading offices; got away the best men, paying them unheard of commissions—made possible, of course, by this Tontine fund. He astounded the public by his lavish advertisements—the money also drawn from the Tontine fund. Into every state and territory his "blue books" found their way. In the early '70's he invaded Europe. His "blue books" appeared in every English parish and every French and German village. Foreigners opened their eyes at this speculative insurance, and, in spite of the frantic protests of the home companies, purchased Tontine policies by the thousand. Thus, in twenty years, by virtue of Tontine, Hyde made the Equitable the biggest life-insurance company in the world. He had accomplished the revenge of his boyhood—had built up a larger company than the Mutual Life. Frederick S. Winston, who shut his door upon young Hyde that eventful March night in 1859, finally died in 1885, disappointed and embittered. At Hyde's own death in 1899 he had accumulated assets of more than $304,000,000, a surplus of more than $65,000,-000, and had more than a billion dollars' worth of insurance in force. He could hardly find a spot on the world's map where the Equitable Society was not known. Americans, Englishmen, Germans, Spaniards, Chinamen, Japanese, and Malay Islanders all entered the mad race for Tontine. He had erected his tremendous monument on the basis of misrepresentations. By this time, too, he had debauched the whole life-insurance system in this country. For how many disap-

pointed lives, how many desolate homes Henry B. Hyde
was responsible; how many millions of dollars he diverted from the hands of their owners into his Tontine pool—these things can never be accurately told.
For his influence extended far beyond the Equitable.
He corrupted not only his own company, but scores of
others. He pursued his scheme so successfully, he accumulated such enormous funds which he used in prop-
agating his own ideas, that the great majority of
companies were forced to follow his example. Twenty
years after he first adopted the Tontine system, four-
fifths of all the other companies had followed suit.
The New York Life fell into line immediately, in 1871 ;
the Mutual, after attacking for years what it called
the " Tontine game," ate its own words after President
Winston's death and became a Tontine company itself.
The Northwestern of Milwaukee fell into line in 1881 ;
the Penn Mutual about the same time. The smaller
New York companies—the Home, the Washington
Life, the Manhattan, the Germania—these were all
forced, many of them say against their will, to become
Tontine companies. Under all sorts of names—reserve
dividend, life rate endowment, dividend investment,
dividend endowment—Tontine became the predominant
idea in American life insurance. Hyde did not win this
great triumph, however, without a hard battle. There

were a few companies and a few men who kept the
faith, who fought, against overwhelming odds, his
demoralising innovations, and who maintained the old
ideals until the end. Only three companies kept themselves entirely free from Tontine; the Mutual Benefit
of New Jersey, the Connecticut Mutual of Hartford,
and the Provident Life and Trust of Philadelphia.
How bravely these opponents struggled, what they
suffered, how they had to wait, for their complete justification, until this year of grace 1906—this story
will be told in the succeeding chapter.

CHAPTER V

THE THIRTY YEARS' WAR

THE Equitable's progress under Tontine caused general consternation among its most conspicuous rivals. They immediately pointed out its injustices, but found themselves unable to stem the popular enthusiasm. Hyde had now obtained what all his rivals desired, but had not had the ingenuity to devise—an unlimited expense fund. While they used all their energies detailing Equitable iniquities and the advantages of old line life insurance, Hyde complacently bought off many of their most effective agents and attracted millions of new business that, under ordinary circumstances, his rivals would have secured.

The Mutual and the New York Life, after fighting the innovation for three years, quietly capitulated. In 1870 the Mutual announced a " new application of the old idea of Tontine "; in 1871 the New York Life advertised a " Tontine Investment Policy." The Mutual adopted the idea somewhat shamefacedly, in deference to what it declared a genuine public sentiment; the New York Life more cheerfully. Indeed, the latter company found it as convenient an escape from embarrassment as did the Equitable itself. Organised in 1841 as a purely mutual company, the New York Life, from the first, had been unfortunate in its management. For many years Pliny Freeman, a thoroughly unscrupulous and dishonest man, had held the chief control. The New York Life, in Freeman's days, paid its dividends, not in cash, but in scrip which bore interest and was subject to redemption at some unspecified date. Freeman acquired the habit of purchasing these scrip dividends on the quiet, at a discount; and then causing the company to cash them in. By other reckless and dishonest methods, he finally, about 1868, brought the company to the verge of insolvency. The trustees, after investigating his management, forced him to resign. Freeman promptly started the Globe Mutual, soon built up, by expensive agency methods, a flourishing company, and then promptly wrecked it.[1]

The trustees selected, as Freeman's successor in the active management, a young blue-eyed clerk in their

[1] Report of John A. McCall, examiner in New York Insurance Department, on the condition of the Globe Mutual Life-Insurance Company (1877): "The results of this investigation conclusively show that, vested with the entire charge of the affairs of this company, as its officers have been, their trust has been wilfully and shamefully abused to their own pecuniary benefit, and to the great injury of the policy-holders."

financial department, whose after career proved one
of the greatest tragedies of life-insurance history.
Of the early life of William H. Beers little is definitely
known. He came of severe Methodist stock, spent several years in the United States Navy, and entered the
New York Life in 1851. Here, by virtue of his energy,
mental alertness, and enthusiasm, he rapidly made his
mark. He fashioned his life-insurance career largely
on the model of Henry B. Hyde. He watched with admiration Hyde's success in the Equitable, and as soon
as he gained control of the New York Life imitated
his methods. In many ways he resembled Hyde. He
had all Hyde's capacity for work; all his devotion to
the company which chiefly owed to him its success.
Largely, too, he had all Hyde's audacity and recklessness. Like Hyde, he lived only in the present; he
esteemed temporary success above stability; and
thought more of new business, "bigness," than the
interest of his insured. "It'll last as long as I do,"
he replied to a subordinate who once called his attention to the flimsy character of his South American
business. He ruled the New York Life as despotically
as Hyde ruled the Equitable. He had a trunk full of
proxies discreetly secreted at his own city house. Once
he filled three executive offices—actuary, secretary, and
vice-president; and, at the same time, rode rough shod

over the nominal president. He ignored not only his policy-holders, but his trustees. He called trustee meetings irregularly, and got together his finance committee only on particular occasions. He supervised the business in all its departments. He practically made all the investments, managed the agency force, and regulated the daily routine. Like Hyde, he depended entirely for the greatness of his company upon the persuasive agent. He engaged anyone who could get business in all its departments. He practically made vanced hundreds of thousands of policy-holders' money to defaulters and notorious gamblers. Brusque and distant with most men, he would pet and fawn upon the successful producer. When John I. D. Bristol, the well-known Northwestern New York manager, demonstrated his capacity in the early '80's, Beers pursued him day and night. " Come, Bristol, with me," he said, throwing his arm around his neck, " and I'll make a millionaire of you." Beers' particular darling was George W. Perkins. He took him as a raw lad, educated him in life-insurance methods, and ultimately transformed him into what, he frequently declared, was the " greatest wonder in the business." He showed no mercy to the unsuccessful man. " What's an agent? " he once declared; " a lemon to be squeezed and thrown away after you have exhausted him."

Beers' craze for new business amounted almost to a disease. To it he ultimately sacrificed himself. His enemies, in 1891, by pointing out his extravagant management, accomplished his destruction. His personal honesty was attacked at the same time, but on this point the evidence was inconclusive. At least he did not die rich.

Beers, a slavish imitator of Hyde's methods, adopted the Tontine idea with enthusiasm. He found in it the same advantages: a method of concealing unfavourable results to policy-holders, and a big expense fund for the purchase of new business. He adopted Hyde's estimate books, and the whole campaign of misrepresentation. He even went to greater extremes; promised policy-holders bigger "investment returns." He clearly outdid Hyde in his advertising methods. He added the bass drum and the cymbals to the life-insurance agents' equipment. He boomed the New York Life in all the colours of the rainbow. Big type, italics, exclamation points, tawdry illustrations, bewildering diagrams—he exhausted every printer's device in emblazoning the glories of Tontine. Competition between the two great Tontine companies soon became animated and unscrupulous. If life insurance had ever been a dignified profession it soon abandoned all pretensions. In the chase for new business Beers never caught up

with Hyde, though in the '80's both left the Mutual
far behind.

In the Mutual Life, indeed, the newfangled life
insurance did not make such startling progress. Above
all, the Mutual aimed at respectability, and its directors rested uneasily under the violent criticisms made
upon Tontine. President Winston never displayed
much enthusiasm for it. He was definitely decided
against it, according to tradition, by a chance meeting with the wife of one of his insured. Her husband,
she said, had foolishly taken out a Tontine policy, had
had reverses and could not make his future payments,
and consequently must lose everything he had put in.
" If it were only a regular policy," she added, " we
might pinch a little and pay the premiums; for then
we could stop any time and get a surrender value; but,
as it is, we must throw the whole thing up." She expressed her opinion of such life insurance in terms that
impressed upon President Winston its iniquity. He decided that it must ultimately become unpopular and
weaken any company that practised it. The Mutual,
therefore, not only abandoned the Tontine policy, but
engaged in a vigorous campaign against it. In advertising circulars and in official reports President Wins-

ton pointed out its injustices and inevitable consequences. The Mutual's criticisms make especially entertaining reading now, inasmuch as, of recent years, it has been one of the foremost advocates of the Tontine principle. Its fallacies and temptations, however, are nowhere more clearly and prophetically pointed out. " In the year 1870," said President Winston in his report for 1873, " the trustees consented to revive, in a modern and scientific form, the old plan of Tontine insurance. . . . But several cases of great hardship were soon forced upon the notice of the company. The plan made it obligatory upon us to forfeit every such policy absolutely and finally, if the premium were not paid upon a certain day, and left us no discretion to consider a claim for a surrender value. This experience satisfied the trustees that the plan, in its nature, is wholly outside the proper range of legitimate life insurance, being little less than a contract by which the company binds itself to execute an unequal wager, securing the stakes to the winner. In such a wager as this, the most needy, whom life insurance is especially designed to protect, are pretty sure to be the losers. Besides, the large accumulations which Tontine insurance gathers in the hands of a company, at the expense of those who die, or are unable to maintain their policies during the Tontine period, offer a strong temptation to wasteful expenditure, which, if indulged, must sooner or later bring disappointment even to the survivors of those who play at Tontine hazard." The Mutual flooded the country with circulars containing similar statements. " The Mutual Life-Insurance Company of New York," declared its most celebrated anti-Tontine document, " issues all kinds of legitimate life and endowment policies, and the premium rates are lower than those of any mutual company in the world. But it does not issue Tontine policies; nor encourage anyone to engage in the Tontine game. The principle of the game is to rob the unfortunate by cancelling their policies without consideration, when it is found impossible to raise the money for premiums; and the object of the game is alleged to be the opportunity for companies which pay very small dividends to conceal the fact for a term of years called a ' Tontine period.' We advise every man to beware of any company which engages in the Tontine game." Again the Mutual declared that Tontine " depends upon speculation in human trouble and misfortune for its ' estimates' of future profit, encourages a gambling instead of a saving habit—boldy intimates that the chances of winning are in favour of the rich—and exposes one of its many cloven feet in its claim to exclusive ownership of a large surplus which should by right belong to

the whole company. In short, Tontine is simply spec-
ulating on the prospective misfortunes of humanity."

Tontine thus precipitated the first great Mutual-
Equitable war. Henry B. Hyde naturally led the
Equitable's forces; Richard A. McCurdy marshalled
the Mutual's hosts. McCurdy at that time had direct
supervision, as vice-president, of the Mutual agency
force. Thus he came into immediate contact with
Hyde, and realised, more keenly than anyone else, his
vigorous and effective competition. In 1872 McCurdy
had not quite reached his fortieth year. In bearing he
was the reverse of Hyde; he had been well-born, carefully educated; had none of the rough and ready manners and willingness to recognise real worth that, in
spite of his many faults, so endeared Hyde to his
associates.

McCurdy regarded Hyde with contempt, as a social
and business inferior, and did not even recognise him
on the street. Like Winston, he looked upon the Equitable as an impertinence; a feeling not at all assuaged
by the remarkable progress it had made. Hyde, the
Mutual's discharged employee, actually wrote more
new business each year than the Mutual Life. From
1868 to 1873 the Equitable issued more policies than
any life-insurance company in the world. At all haz-
ards McCurdy decided to humiliate the youthful giant.

The favourite weapon of life-insurance warfare,
then as now, was the defamatory circular. The companies printed these by the thousand and placed them
in the agents' hands for use on critical occasions.
These circulars had one great advantage: they were
seldom issued as official documents, were anonymous,
and thus, in case of necessity, could be easily disavowed.
McCurdy, in 1872, started a circular campaign against
the Equitable. He put in printed form the current
Equitable scandals, accused it of all manner of frauds
and outrages, and attacked, with special severity, its
new form of policy.[2] Hyde, it may be supposed, did
not remain inactive. He had spent several years in the
Mutual's office, and knew its weak points even better
than McCurdy himself. He found a valuable ally in
one Stephen English, at that time editor and pro-
prietor of the most ably conducted insurance paper
of the day. English was a wild Irish adventurer. He
had served as chief of police at Leeds and Norwich,
England, and, emigrating in the latter '60's, had

[2] Testimony of Richard A. McCurdy before the Insurance
Committee of the New York Legislature in 1877 (page 315).

Q. You published pamphlets of what you claimed were frauds
and outrages perpetrated by the Equitable? A. Yes, sir; we
published a good many lively documents at that time.

Q. Well, about how large a number? A. Just as many as
I could get out—just as many as I could think of.

plunged into insurance journalism. As a writer on life-insurance topics he ranked far ahead of the venal blackmailers who then so largely infested the insurance press. In a few years he became the terror of the insurance world. When not pounding away at solvent concerns, he was singing the praises of dishonest ones. He did his best to ruin the Connecticut Mutual, always a tower of honesty; and was a leading journalistic supporter of the Universal, the most scandalous fraud of the time. For several years, up to 1872, he had had only honeyed words for the Mutual Life. He publicly boasted that he was its " organ." He personally acted as Winston's representative at proxy elections, and hounded any man who breathed the slightest criticism of the Mutual's management. Then suddenly, for no publicly explained reason, he turned his broadsides against them. Observers noted that his change of heart coincided with Hyde's onslaught on the Mutual, and that the advertising patronage of the Equitable and the New York Life perceptibly increased.

A MUTUAL INVESTIGATION OF 1870

The Mutual openly charged Hyde with instigating these attacks. In ferocity they far surpassed McCurdy's onslaught on the Equitable. English had, as we have seen, abundant material. Winston's " bonuses," his dead son's revived policies, his loans to his trustees, his favouritism to his relatives, his corruption of the legislature and the insurance department—all these were matters of official record. In 1870 the Superintendent of Insurance, George W. Miller, and James W. McCulloh, a special representative of the New York Assembly, investigated the Mutual. They uncovered all these things and many more. McCulloh displayed such industry, indeed, that the Mutual, in spite of the fact that he represented the Assembly, prohibited his further access to the books. "There has been far too much leakage here," declared Winston. In face of all these disclosures, Superintendent Miller submitted a whitewashing report, which the Mutual spread broadcast as a complete vindication. Some years afterward, the Mutual admitted on the witness stand that they had paid Miller $2500 for this report. They not only got a favourable report, but compelled Miller to suppress the official testimony. The Mutual furnished their own stenographer, and, after the investigation ceased, copyrighted the minutes. They took this method of suppressing the damaging evidence the officers had given against themselves. McCulloh obtained a copy and was threatened with prosecution if he made public use of it. Miller took the official copy up to Albany, and it has never been seen since. Superintendent Hendricks made a thorough search for the present writer and reported that it was not in his archives. It was located finally at the Library of Congress, where it was deposited, of course, to protect the copyright.[*] If Superintendent Hendricks' recent investigation of the Equitable Life had been officially suppressed, and if the Equitable had copyrighted all the testimony and thus prohibited its public use, we should have had a proceeding precisely parallel with that engineered by the Mutual Life thirty-five years ago. Miller was the only one who suffered because of this high-handed proceeding. It, and similar financial transactions with other companies, cost him his official position. One of his appointments to office in the insurance department, it is now interesting to note, was that of John A. McCall, then an obscure Albany politician.

[*] "Examination of Witness Before George W. Miller, Esq., Superintendent of the Insurance Department of the State of New York. In relation to certain charges against the officers and trustees of the Mutual Life-Insurance Company of New York. Entered, according to Act of Congress, in the year 1870, by the Mutual Life-Insurance Company of New York. In the clerk's office of the District Court of the United States for the Southern District of New York."

A MARTYR TO FREE SPEECH

In so viciously attacking Hyde, the Mutual thus treaded on dangerous ground. Someone evidently furnished English a copy of this suppressed testimony, for he used it tellingly. McCurdy and Winston then tried another tack. They told Hyde that, if he didn't cease his onslaught, they would reduce their premium rates. In the latter part of 1873 they made good this threat. Their own policy-holders now took sides with Hyde and English. They held public meetings all over the country, and, at times, stormed the offices of the Mutual Life in New York. They objected to being used as clubs with which to attack the Equitable. They declared that the Mutual, in lowering its rates, had threatened its own stability. Above all, the old policy-holders objected to paying the full premiums while new members got in at a 25 per cent. reduction. They made things so warm for Winston that he finally withdrew the schedule. English renewed his assaults; the exchange of defamatory circulars still went on. In a moment of desperation Winston had a charge of criminal libel lodged against English. The doughty editor fled to Jersey City, but in an unguarded moment returned to New York, and was nabbed by the police and rushed into Ludlow Street Jail. Winston sued him on a multitude of charges, and caused him to be held on $80,000 bail. English naturally could not furnish sureties to this amount and spent more than six months in prison, awaiting trial.

These proceedings set the whole town into an uproar. English, in a way, became a popular hero. He edited his newspaper from his cell, attacking Winston more violently than before. He pictured himself as a martyr to the cause of free speech, and declared that the Mutual Life had sought to gag him. In the public mind the matter now assumed greater proportions than the mere personalities of those engaged. Attention centred upon the incarceration, by the most powerful corporation of the day, of a comparatively uninfluential citizen; and upon the fact that it persistently refused to bring the man to trial. There was a strong conviction that English, whatever his motives or personal shortcomings, had told the truth. English became a popular theme with those who preached against the growing power and arrogance of corporations. The Assembly sent down a committee to investigate. It held many sessions, took a large amount of testimony, and submitted a report entirely favourable to English and entirely unfavourable to the Mutual Life.* It virtually declared that nearly everything English had written against the Mutual was true. English's im-

* New York Assembly Document 155: 1873.

prisonment, it added, was a just cause of "grievance and a proper subject of relief"; and it declared that Winston's chances of obtaining damages against him were exceedingly remote. The Mutual Life now faced a most embarrassing situation. English, still in jail, attacked it with renewed enthusiasm; the Equitable diligently scattered broadcast, with the aid of its agents, the Assembly's report against it. It's business fell off rapidly; in one year it lost $17,000,000 of new insurance.

Winston now approached Hyde with a flag of truce. The Mutual promised in the future to let the Equitable alone, if Hyde would only quiet the editor of the *Insurance Times*. As McCurdy expressed it: "Hyde called off his dog and we called off ours." [5] Hyde also

[5] New York Insurance Investigation, 1877 (p. 315).

Testimony of Richard A. McCurdy.

Q. Was not this settlement between English and your company brought about by the intervention of Mr. Hyde, president of the Equitable? A. That is only presumption on my part; I was waging war on the other side, and I was not a party to the compromise and was very reluctant to have it made.

Q. Was it not a fact that the war between your company and English and the war between your company and the Equitable, ceased at the same time? A. Yes, sir.

Q. And Mr. Hyde was regarded as the backer of English as against your company? A. He was.

Q. This arrangement or compromise was brought about, as you understood it, by Hyde having to quiet English and the whole thing stopped? A. Well, he called off his dog and we called off ours.

had had enough, for his business had also suffered. He bore to English, however, more than merely President Winston's apology. He handed him a sum of money sufficient to assuage his wounded feelings and reimburse him for his incarceration. English himself admitted, on the witness stand, that he had been paid money, but declined to state the amount.[6] Afterward when asked frequently what reason he had for dropping his fight against the Mutual he always jocularly replied: " I had thirty-five thousand reasons." Released from jail he at once became a warm defender of the Mutual. He waxed rich on the patronage of the Mutual and other large companies. He lived in a large and beautiful house in Brooklyn, and, when not fighting the battles of the New York companies, spent an elegant leisure cultivating strawberries and collecting etchings.

[6] Ibid (page 437).

Testimony of Stephen English.

Q. Were you paid anything, or agreed to be paid anything, by or on behalf of Mr. Winston on that subject? A. For false imprisonment, loss of business, loss of property and everything else, yes.

Q. How much? A. I don't know that I have the right to mention how much.

(Question ordered withdrawn by the Committee after a long wrangle.)

MUTUAL BEGINS TO REBATE—OFFICIALLY

This peace, however, proved only temporary. All through the '70's the warfare burst forth repeatedly. It was a trying period for Winston and the Mutual. Every day the Equitable gained upon its older rival. Hyde purchased Mutual agents right and left; its entire agency system, according to President Winston's own words, threatened to become " so impaired that years would be required to restore its efficiency." Rebating now became a regular feature of life-insurance competition. This, it may be explained, is the agent's practice of dividing his first year's commission with the new policy-holder. This custom, now one of the greatest scandals of the business, is the direct outcome of the Mutual-Equitable warfare of the '70's. Hyde, by paying such enormous commissions on first year's business, made it possible for the agent to pay back a good part to the insured and still make a fair profit himself. The Mutual withstood the strain for some years; and then went the Equitable one better. In the fall of 1878 Winston and McCurdy issued a famous pronunciamento, publicly offering a 30 per cent. rebate, on first and second premiums, to all new policy-holders. Rebating had become so open, they declared, that any attempt at concealment was absurd; instead of letting the agent make the rebate, they therefore proposed that the company do it directly. Similarly amazing were the instructions given the agents. The Mutual authorised the acceptance of a demand note for this 30 per cent. rebate. If the applicant expressed anxiety that he might actually be held liable for this note, the agent was to quiet him by writing " without recourse " before the signature. " But," added the Mutual, " *do not do this unless it shall be absolutely required.*" In other words, the agents were directed to trick the policy-holder into giving a good note, if possible; if not, why then to accept a fictitious one. Winston succeeded only in making the Mutual ridiculous. There was then as much public sentiment against rebating as now; and the offer of the largest and oldest and most dignified company to do the thing itself was too much for the national sense of humour. Winston was soon obliged to withdraw the plan. He was now in his eightieth year; the decreasing importance of the Mutual and the steady growth of the Equitable were embittering his old age. As a final checkmate, he again reduced his premium rates 15 per cent. Hyde only laughed at him. His official reply was an increase of his agents' commissions, and another raid on the Mutual's force. The public preferred the higher-priced speculative insurance to the lower-priced old-fashioned article. A year or two after the Mutual cut its rates the Equitable wrote twice as much new business.

Winston's battle had its pathetic and its creditable side. Unfortunate as many of his official acts had been, in the main he upheld conservatism. He would not advance the Mutual by the reckless methods adopted by Hyde. Every move the Equitable made, President Winston opposed. In 1873 Hyde invaded Europe; a few years later, South America. Winston promptly and accurately pointed out the dangers of the innovation, and declared that the Mutual would never follow suit. "Other companies may go to the West Indies, Central and South America," said President Winston in an official report, "but not the Mutual. It is not fair to introduce risks on bad lives, especially when exposed to deleterious climatic influences. The rate of exchange greatly interferes with the transmission of funds; executive powers cannot be safely deputed to agents; the remoteness of the field of action offers temptations to frauds; the customs and usages of foreign countries would often render compliance therewith a matter of extravagant cost. The home field affords ample scope for the exercise of whatever capacity and energy any company may possess." Again President Winston frequently argued against that

besetting sin of the modern life-insurance company—
the craze for size. In 1874 the Mutual announced that
it would issue policies only up to 100,000 lives; after
that, take new risks only to fill such vacancies as occurred. Winston constantly attacked the Equitable's
huge surplus. " These accumulations," he said, " instead of being a surplus adding to the security of the
general policy-holder, are simply unpaid or deferred
dividends, withheld from the special beneficiaries, not
to be directed to the use or benefit of the general policy-
holder without a breach of trust." In other words,
Winston scored nearly every life-insurance idea which
the Mutual has since conspicuously made its own. He
died in 1885; Richard A. McCurdy promptly succeeded him. McCurdy at once surrendered to Hyde.
He converted the Mutual Life into another Equitable.
He made the Mutual a Tontine company, and established agencies abroad. He entered the race for bigness, and began heaping up that huge surplus against
which President Winston had so strongly and truth-
fully preached. He showed even less moderation than
Hyde himself. By using Hyde's methods he built up
an enormous company, but at tremendous cost to Mutual policy-holders. Since 1885 dividends in the Mutual
Life have regularly diminished.

AMZI DODD

Elsewhere the battle against Tontine still went furiously on. In Jacob L. Greene, President of the Connecticut Mutual of Hartford, and in Amzi Dodd, President of the Mutual Benefit of New Jersey, old line life insurance found vigorous and successful champions. Under Mr. Greene the Connecticut Mutual not only refused to follow the New York example, but fought it wherever it appeared. Jacob L. Greene was fitted by intellect and temperament for the great part he was now called upon to play. He was born on an upland farm in Maine, received his early education at a district school, and prepared for the bar at the University of Michigan. He early enlisted as a sergeant in the Civil War, saw much action, was brevetted lieutenant colonel for " distinguished gallantry " at the battle of Trevillian Station, and spent several months in Libby Prison. When the war ended he entered life insurance as an agent for the Berkshire Life-Insurance Company, soon became its secretary, and in 1871 went to the Connecticut Mutual. Here he rose rapidly, and, in 1878, became its president. He had a marked aptitude for mathematics, and had written largely and well upon certain broad life-insurance questions.

Mr. Greene acquired the leadership of the Connecticut Mutual at a critical time. His company had started in 1846, when a few citizens of Connecticut associated themselves for mutual life-insurance protection; and it had always stood as a living embodiment of New England industry and thrift. When Mr. Greene entered its service it ranked next in size to the Mutual Life; the Equitable and the New York Life had only about half its assets. In the financial panic of 1873 the Connecticut Mutual had suffered seriously in its real estate investments, and had to purchase at foreclosure a large amount of mortgaged property—of which fact its competitors always made the most malicious use. Again, when Mr. Greene assumed control, the country had just passed through a life-insurance panic. Not far from thirty companies in New York State alone had collapsed; the grossest frauds in their management had been disclosed; life insurance, like the railroads, had its Jay Goulds and its Jim Fisks; their wrecking, for the purpose of private profit, had become a staple industry. Demonstrated rascality, gross mismanagement and extravagance, had shaken public confidence in the whole institution. Hardly any company escaped; the Equitable was commonly declared to be insolvent; the strength of the Mutual was called in question. In face of this experience, few companies

showed any disposition to reform. Hardly had the
storm subsided when, under the leadership of Hyde,
they plunged into new excesses. "In the future,"
declared Frederick S. Winston, " the struggle will be
between conservatism and audacity."

In 1878 President Greene thus stood at the parting
of the ways. He faced a clearly defined issue. He had,
on the one hand, the option of adopting all the New
York methods—high commissions and salaries to
agents, reckless advertising, great office buildings,
the pursuit of foreign business at the expense of the
American members, the adoption of new speculative
forms of insurance. In that direction lay success, as
most Americans then esteemed success. Thus, and thus
only, could Greene maintain the comparative size and
assets of the Connecticut Mutual. In this way, of
course, he would greatly prejudice his old policy-
holders; make their insurance more expensive. On the
other hand, Greene could maintain all the old tradi-
tions; keep foremost in mind the interests of his present members; furnish them life insurance at its lowest
cost consistent with absolute safety; maintain in its
integrity the mutual principle; refuse to increase
his agents' commissions; and refrain from popular
innovations. In that direction, however, lay apparent
failure. Thus would President Greene sacrifice his

company's standing as one of the "big three," and drop from second, perhaps to fourth, fifth, or sixth place. Mr. Greene did not hesitate. He put aside success obtained at the great price then demanded; deliberately relegated his company to a subordinate position, judged by the standards of mere size; and for more than thirty years remained the foremost defender of conservative ideas.

Life insurance was part of Mr. Greene's very being. It was not an occupation, a business; it was a religion. He viewed it in its broad social and moral aspects. It saved millions to the state in the prevention of pauperism; therefore it was a powerful factor in social economy. It was a monument to family affection; therefore it conduced to public morals. It was made possible only by family co-operation, by the joining of the many to bear the burdens of the few; therefore it represented, as did no other institution, human brotherhood. Above all, it rested upon absolutely secure scientific grounds; it was thus a product of human progress in intelligence. In the conduct of his company Jacob L. Greene constantly kept these ideas in mind. Rivalry among companies, except rivalry in best promoting these aims, he detested. He regarded, and properly, the position of a life company as identical with that of a university: an institution engaged, not in money

JACOB L. GREENE

making, in promoting the private interests of its trustees, but in disseminating public benefits. In his eyes a life-insurance president who used his position for private enrichment should be regarded as would be a university president who speculated with the university funds. He regarded life insurance simply as a family protection; on the part of the insured, he declared again and again, it was a purely unselfish act. No policy-holder must himself expect to benefit from his policy. He opposed all innovations not conducive to this end. At times, in carrying out this idea, he went to what many reputable authorities deemed extremes. Thus, he took a strong stand against the cash surrender system. He declared that, once a man had entrusted to his keeping certain sums for his family protection, the insured had no right to withdraw them. The company had accepted this money as a trustee, and under no conditions must it use it for any other than the intended purpose—that is, life insurance. Should poverty prevent the payment of premiums, Greene believed that the accumulation should be used only in buying a paid-up policy. Once insured, always insured, was his motto.

The company's function, from Greene's point of view, was limited simply to providing this family protection at its mathematically ascertained cost. He stood powerfully for the mutual idea. For a company to discriminate among its members, to furnish some life insurance cheaper than the rest—this was the crowning evil. Naturally his soul revolted from the Tontine system, which was based upon forfeitures and the enrichment of the more fortunate at the expense of the poor. Mutuality was also violated when new members were admitted at the expense of the old. He refused to purchase new business with the dividends of those already in. He paid such low agents' commissions and made what were regarded as such illiberal agents' contracts that he had the utmost difficulty in getting efficient men. While Hyde, Beers, and McCurdy paid large salaries and 50 or 75 per cent. of the first premium and handsome renewals, Greene offered 30 per cent., with no guarantee of renewals at all. While the New York companies advanced hundreds of thousands of dollars on commissions, Greene refused to advance a single penny. He had no contract that he could not break at will; and, in case an agent died, his interests in commissions died with him. Greene's ambition was, not big commissions to his agents, but big dividends to his insured. Again, he rebelled against certain " liberal " ideas introduced by Tontine companies—notably their so-called " incontestable policies." He regarded the payment of the claims of suicides as a violation of the mutual idea. He declared that a man who, unless insane, committed suicide in order to benefit his family, did precisely as the man who fired his house in order to collect the fire insurance: he practised a fraud upon his associate insurers. The act was, Greene declared, " the very essence of swindling," and " as destructive of public morals as of honest contract obligations." He regarded the departure of a New York company, in offering to pay a suicide's claim the day after issuing the policy, as one of the most immoral acts ever promulgated in the name of life insurance.

NEW YORK-HARTFORD WARFARE

When Hyde began his campaign he found the Connecticut Mutual, next to the Mutual Life, his most formidable competitor. Naturally he opened his broadsides against it. He used the tactics so effective against the Mutual Life. There was hardly one of the Connecticut Mutual's leading agents, declared Greene, who had not received offers from New York. In the latter '70's and early '80's Hyde formed an offensive and defensive alliance with the Mutual and the New York Life for the purpose of crushing their Hartford rival. There is no more shameful chapter in our financial history than the hounding that followed. They distributed broadcast circulars and pamphlets; but, above all, they used the New York insurance press. Several leading insurance papers started a campaign of wholesale abuse against the Hartford company. C. C. Hine, editor of the *Insurance Monitor*, and our old friend Stephen English, editor of the *Insurance Times*, led the assault. Charles J. Smith, editor of the *Insurance Record*—that same Smith who figured in the recent New York insurance investigation, as the maker of public opinion, at a dollar a line, favourable to the Mutual Life—played an active, though less conspicuous, part. For several years these insurance journalists made a specialty of the Connecticut Mutual. They filled column after column, issue after issue, with the wildest abuse. At times they had little else in their papers. They even issued " extras " devoted entirely to the Hartford company. They assaulted Greene personally. Because he refused to adopt the modern methods, they described him as an " old fogy "; because he wrote, for several years, a decreasing amount of new business, they called him incompetent. They cartooned him, assailed him in doggerel verse, and called upon the policy-holders to eject him from office. They attacked the solvency of the Connecticut Mutual itself. They found a choice morsel in its foreclosed real estate. They even had valuations made of it, and published these as sure proof that the company had gone to the wall.

The editor of the *Insurance Monitor* declared, in his own columns, that he had sold copies of his paper containing these attacks "by the ton." His standing price for his Connecticut Mutual extras was $50 a thousand. The purchasers made little attempt to conceal their identity. Greene openly charged that the Equitable and the Mutual prepared many of the articles in their own offices. He named particular authors of particular articles. That they remained for years the favourite canvassing documents of Equitable, Mutual, and New York Life agents was notorious. Connecticut Mutual policy-holders were inundated; leading citizens of American cities were overwhelmed. Anyone even mildly contemplating life insurance inevitably received, through the mail, a marked copy of the *Monitor* or the *Times*. Many of these articles were found mailed in Equitable envelopes. Greene, over his own signature, charged that the New York companies had spent $500,000 hounding the Connecticut Mutual.

President Greene met all these attacks in the open. He replied directly to Henry B. Hyde, Richard A. McCurdy, and William H. Beers. He did not assault the companies or the men, but their methods. He regarded himself as a chosen instrument to expose existing life-insurance quackeries. He discussed, in his annual reports, not only his own company, but the

whole philosophy of life insurance. He attacked the
very evils which have recently occupied the public mind.
In particular he exposed Tontine insurance. He denounced it as gambling, as thus subversive of public
morals; as merely a scheme for accumulating a large
expense fund and enriching life-insurance managers
and stock-holders. "Where in human history," he
asked, "has so enormous a game been attempted or
conceived? What colossal gambling! For what a peculiar stake—the protection, the living of widows and
children! . . . The results by which life insurance
is to stand at the last will be the amount of protection
given to families, not the amount of which they have
been robbed, not the profits it has been made to yield
in a game of chance, nor the magnitude of the game
which has been set going in its name." He wielded a
caustic pen. In 1892 the New York companies appealed
for a law restricting the amount of new business they
could write each year—though not, as it afterward
turned out, in good faith. "This reminds one," said
Greene, "of the debauchee who asks to be put under
restraint until he can recover sobriety and self-con-
trol." He ridiculed the "costly advertisements in a
multitude of papers whose ignorant praise is dearly
paid for." He riddled the Tontine estimates, showing
by mathematics that they never could be made good.

" Companies whose premiums are eaten up by extravagance," he declared, " hold out the prospect of unexam-
pled returns of surplus. But," he added, " the glitter
of big figures quite overbears such sober facts as the
multiplication table and the moral law."

GREENE DECLINES TO COMPROMISE

About 1885 the New York-Hartford war became
·particularly lively. Greene carried his case into the
newspapers. His long letters in the *New York Tribune*,
pointing out the tendencies of Tontine, created a great
public sensation. Hyde, McCurdy, and Beers replied
through the same medium. They now repeated, over
their own signatures, practically all the slanders the
insurance journals had spread broadcast for years.
They attacked Greene personally, attributing his criticisms to professional jealousy; called attention to his
comparatively small amount of new business, and
broadly intimated that his company was insolvent.
Greene replied vigorously. The discussion aroused the
greatest public interest; the letters, on both sides,
were generally republished; the public, for the first
time, began discussing Tontine. Two legislatures, New
York and Ohio, appointed committees of investigation
—the result of which will be described subsequently.
Business was affected; policy-holders began to turn

away from Tontine. In fact, Hyde and McCurdy thoroughly tired of the subject, and sought some way of stopping the discussion. In the early part of 1886 Greene sent a four-column letter to a leading New York paper. The editor forwarded a proof to the Equitable, inviting a rejoinder. The Equitable threw up its hands. It had had enough. It consulted with the Mutual as to the best way of ending the war. They finally sent for James G. Batterson, President of the Travellers Insurance Company of Hartford. Couldn't Mr. Batterson call Greene off? Above all, couldn't he persuade Greene not to publish that letter? If Greene would only keep quiet, they promised to cease their ten years' onslaught. If Greene would stop exposing Tontine, Hyde and his associates would pledge their word never again to attack the Connecticut Mutual. They authorised Mr. Batterson to make this proposition in so many words.

President Batterson returned to Hartford and delivered the message. He and Greene were never afterward friends. The latter ordered his letter printed, and followed it with another, describing the attempts made to shut him off. His attacks, he declared, had not been started for the purpose of purchasing immunity, but to discharge what he regarded as an important public duty. " I will not stop," he declared in an open

letter to the New York presidents, " until I have done
that which I believe my duty, to wit: to thoroughly
inform those, the welfare of whose families is involved,
as to an abstruse matter which I know they do not
understand, and which I think I do; and I must leave
with you the responsibility for continuing or stopping
the attacks upon the Connecticut Mutual and myself
as you may deem best for the interest of your companies and yourselves, the good of the public, and the
benefit of legitimate life insurance." He was as good
as his word. Until the day of his death President Greene
hammered away at Tontine. To a great extent, however, the public forgot his preachings. That he was
eternally right is now only too clearly apparent. The
New York legislature has recently enacted into law
practically all the reforms for which the Hartford
president contended. One of the most pathetic episodes
in the recent situation was the death of Jacob L.
Greene just as his hard-fought battle had been won.
He died in March, 1905, on the eve of the Equitable
upheaval.

AMZI DODD'S EFFORTS FOR REFORM

In Newark, Amzi Dodd also stood for many years
a foremost advocate of legitimate life-insurance methods. Like Greene, Mr. Dodd was both a mathematician

and a lawyer. He had served for many years as vice-chancellor of New Jersey and had also figured conspicuously in public affairs. He joined the Mutual Benefit Life in 1863; held the position of mathematician from 1865 to 1882, and the presidency from 1882 to 1901. In that period he stamped his personality and his convictions upon his company. He took a firm stand for the mutual idea. Like Greene, he opposed the new theories promulgated by the Equitable. He combated the idea that mere figures signified; he refused to write business not only abroad, but in certain parts of the United States which he regarded as unsound. As far back as 1878 he demanded reform in agency management; extravagance, he declared, was one of the greatest menaces to life insurance. Like Greene, he had to meet unscrupulous competition. The New York companies never attacked the Mutual Benefit quite so viciously, but they constantly raided its agency force and indulged in the usual literary campaign against it. Dodd was not so combative as Greene; he did not hesitate, however, to fight for his convictions. He sharply criticised the Mutual Life's official rebate plan of 1878. In particular, he scored the Mutual Life for its illiberal treatment of lapsing policy-holders.

Dodd's great contribution to life insurance is the

non-forfeiture plan adopted by the Mutual Benefit in
1879. His company, compared with the standards of
the time, had always shown much conscience in the
treatment of lapsing members. Dodd's attention was directed to it from the first. His earliest reports as mathematician pointed out the need of reform. Naturally he
abhorred the Tontine system. Hyde had made forfeitures the very foundation of his society. Dodd promptly
went to the other extreme. He made non-forfeiture the
prevailing idea of the Mutual Benefit. Hyde sought
every opportunity to confiscate the equities of his retiring members; Dodd adopted a plan by which such
injustice became impossible. In 1879 he offered the
lapsing member two options: a paid-up policy in exchange for his reserve, or the application of the reserve
in the payment of premiums upon the old policy. He
extended this privilege not only to new but to old
policy-holders. That is, he refused to take advantage
of the forfeiture clauses written before the days of
enlightenment. Again, his plan worked automatically.
Lapsing policy-holders, up to that time, had been
obliged formally to notify the company that they expected a surrender value. If they neglected this for-
mality, they received nothing at all. This provision
frequently worked great hardships. On no subject has
ignorance so generally prevailed as in life insurance;

and people by the thousands dropped their policies, unaware that they were entitled to any return. Others, through illness, unexpected absence, sudden insanity, or carelessness, failed to send such notifications. Dodd, therefore, provided in every policy that, if the lapsing member selected no option, his reserve would be used until exhausted in continuing annual premiums on his policy. That was, no man could forfeit his policy however hard he tried. Many bereaved widows have been amazed to receive checks, in payment of policies, from the Mutual Benefit Life-Insurance Company. Their husbands had formerly carried policies, they knew, but supposed that they had dropped them years before. . Amzi Dodd, unknown to them, had taken the reserve value, at lapse, and applied it to continue premiums. Whenever the insured died before this money was exhausted the full face of the policy was always paid. In working out the details of these reforms Mr. Bloomfield J. Miller, the late mathematician of the Mutual Benefit, shares the credit with Amzi Dodd.

Mr. Dodd did not go to such extremes as President Greene. He did not share the latter's views on cash values, suicides' claims, or even on the management of the agency force. He made no hysterical bids for new business; he did desire, however, a steady and healthy growth. He would not meet the high commissions paid in New York, but he did pay slightly more than Greene, and made more popular agents' contracts. His company thus acquired the reputation of being progressive without adopting the excesses of the time. Thus Amzi Dodd succeeded where Greene had failed; he increased the size of his company. He also kept the Mutual Benefit free from scandal. His strength was clearly brought out in 1896, when the Republican National campaign committee called upon the Mutual Benefit, as upon all the large insurance companies, for a contribucion. The usual arguments were made—the moral issues involved, the duty of protecting the policy-holders' assets from depletion, and so on. It was a time of great excitement, and high-minded men might readily be led astray. The venerable president, however, brushed aside all sophistries of this kind. If the Mutual Benefit Board must subscribe, he declared, let them subscribe as individuals, out of their own pockets, but not a penny of the policy-holders' money must be touched. Thus the Republican party had to worry along without financial assistance from this source.

CHAPTER VI

THE RAID ON THE SURPLUS

IN the early '80's the Tontine bubble burst. The first policies reached maturity; and the Equitable was called upon to make good its agents' promises. As all the authorities had anticipated and predicted, it paid the surviving members only small proportions of its estimates. Its failure, indeed, was even greater than general expectation; and unexplainable on the grounds apologetically put forth.

From that time the Equitable has been called upon annually to redeem its pledges and has invariably failed. A few quotations from its own official publications sufficiently illustrate its deficiencies. In 1871, for example, the Equitable issued to one " J. B." [1] aged forty-three, a $10,000 policy maturing in 1886. The agent estimated that Mr. " J. B." would obtain, at the end of his Tontine period, cash " profits " of $5328. In fact, the Equitable paid him $2931. In the same year it issued a $25,000 policy to one " J. S. T.," [2] also

[1] Results of Tontine policies maturing in 1886. Page 11, Equitable Official Document.
[2] Ibid. Page 10.

maturing in fifteen years. The agent estimated cash
profits of $12,142.50. The Equitable paid $6693.50.
Thousands of similar instances could be specified. In
general, the Equitable has seldom paid more than sixty
per cent. of the estimated profits. It has averaged in
the neighbourhood of fifty, and frequently has ultimately paid only forty and thirty. The other New
York companies have made records similarly bad. The
Northwestern Mutual, although it also has failed to
realise its anticipations, has made a much better showing. The Northwestern has held itself to a strict
accountability. While the New York companies have
gone to extremes to avoid accounting, and have
paid at the conclusion of the Tontine periods whatever
winnings they chose, the Northwestern has willingly
rendered precise statements to every policy-holder every
year. Dishonesty, under these conditions, was practically impossible.

Statistics give no adequate idea of the sufferings
these Tontine settlements involved. Hyde's comparatively small dividends were realised by forfeiting the
policies of unnumbered smaller and more unfortunate
members. Mr. " J. S. T.," whose record is quoted above,
represented a class especially attracted by the Tontine
scheme. He was evidently a man of large means. The
New York companies have always preached Tontine,

on the ground that many men were thus persuaded to insure who ordinarily would not have taken out policies at all. Such men, that is, entered the company, not for the insurance, but for the "investment." In other words, men of wealth have taken Tontine policies in order to get the profits made by closing out those less affluent than themselves. In 1878 Elizur Wright declared that, up to date, 100,000 policy-holders in the Equitable and New York Life, who had dropped their policies, " found themselves in no better position than if the companies had failed." In 1885 John K. Tarbox, insurance commissioner of Massachusetts, declared that forfeitures already set apart and divided under the Tontine system " would have provided for dependent family support to the amount of tens of millions of dollars." In the main, lapsing members were those overtaken by misfortune. Others ceased through carelessness, misunderstandings concerning the days of payment or days of grace allowed, or temporary illness. Others had taken Tontines with inadequate notions of what they were, and then afterward abandoned them in disgust. Many, in the hope of inordinate gain, had taken much larger policies than their circumstances justified, and after paying several large premiums, dropped out. All, of course, had absolutely no redress.

However, the lot of the survivors was almost as un-

fortunate. The great majority had accepted the agents'
estimates as absolute guarantees. Thousands had
adopted this method of providing for old age. Inevitably, when they found themselves so badly deceived,
they sought redress.   They bombarded the Equitable
and the New York Life with protests, and personally
stormed the offices. They obtained little satisfaction.
Hyde, Beers, and the rest repudiated all the agents'
promises, and triumphantly pointed out that the estimates had never been incorporated in the policy. Again,
they called attention to the clause that virtually forced
the acceptance of any apportionment made. For the
next twenty years the policy-holders sought satisfaction in several ways. Through legislative investigations
they tried to penetrate the Tontine secret. In 1885 the
Ohio legislature authorised a committee to investigate
Tontine. The New York Companies forced upon it, as
consulting actuary, Mr. Sheppard Homans, the man
who, above all others, devised the Tontine system and
compiled the Tontine estimates. Homans led the committee by the nose. He held many of the sessions in his
own office, and examined practically all the witnesses
himself. The proceedings developed into merely a congress of presidents and actuaries, who, day after day,
loudly sang hosannahs to Tontine. In New York, public sentiment, largely aroused by Jacob L. Greene's

attacks, forced the appointment of a Tontine committee. The legislature limited the sessions practically
to four days, and refused to authorise the employment
of counsel. The first session, held at the Fifth Avenue
Hotel, developed into a farce. William B. Hornblower,
as counsel for the New York Life, and Charles C. Bea-
man, as counsel for the Equitable, consumed most of
the time by asking meaningless questions; Chauncey M.
Depew dropped in and told a few humorous stories.
The committee subpœnæd Henry B. Hyde, but he had
mysteriously left town. James W. Alexander appeared
as the leading witness. The committee demanded certain
important Equitable books, but Mr. Alexander gently
postponed their presentation. It asked for the Equitable's salary list, and that Mr. Alexander also diplo-
matically withheld. He did, however, reveal several
interesting facts. He declared that the Equitable directors had never authorised the Tontine policy; at least,
that no record of such authorisation existed. He added
that the idea that Tontines were kept in classes was a
" popular delusion." For years the Equitable, in num-
berless official documents, had maintained that such
classes existed; and Henry B. Hyde, under oath on
the witness-stand in 1877, had repeated the statement.
The committee asked Mr. Alexander how the Tontine
results were arrived at. " It is something of a puzzle,"

he replied, "to know just how the adjustment is reached." The four days having expired, the committee returned to Albany and asked for an extension of time. Senator James Husted, for years the leader of the insurance lobby, now took charge and prevented this extension. The legislature even attempted to shut off an official report. In 1887 Theodore M. Banta, the present cashier of the New York Life, informed his board that its share of the expense incurred in quieting this investigation was $7500. ·

" RED-INK " TONTINES

All attempts to kill Tontine by legislation, the New York companies successfully opposed. If a law actually got upon the statute books, they usually discovered some way of nullifying it. Only one thing could kill the Tontine scheme: a law which, like that of Massachusetts, prohibited the forfeiture of policies. All through the '70's insurance reformers sought to imitate, in New York State, this Massachusetts legislation. In the year 1879 public sentiment proved too strong and actually forced a surrender value law through the legislature. This guaranteed lapsing policy-holders the value of at least two-thirds the reserve, either in temporary or paid-up insurance. In that form it would have ended the Tontine policy; Hyde and his asso-

ciates, therefore, appended an amendment which authorised policies with no surrender values, provided they
contained on the margin a notice printed *in red ink* that
all rights to such surrender values had been waived.
Recent legislation on patent medicines permits their
sale provided the ingredients are duly labelled on the
bottle. Likewise, the legislature now authorised Tontine, provided the prescriptions were printed on the
margin. The New York Life circumvented this red-ink
clause in characteristic fashion. President Beers issued
a policy in which not only the waiver clause, but numerous other sections, were printed in red ink. By spatter-
ing red ink all over the policy the New York Life
diverted attention from the damaging clause the law
required.

HYDE SECURES IMMUNITY FROM LAW SUITS

The policy-holders, failing to obtain satisfaction in
the legislature or through investigating committees,
now appealed to the courts. An avalanche of lawsuits
started against the Equitable and the New York Life.
Policy-holders alleged fraud, misrepresentation, and
failure to keep proper accountings of regular Tontine
classes. At times the companies quieted prospective liti-
gants, especially if they were influential citizens, by
increasing the Tontine payments. In some instances

they even silenced popular clamour by settling Tontine policies before the periods had expired. In 1887, for example, the New York Life purchased a $100,000 policy on the life of John V. Farwell, of Chicago, for $40,000. Mr. Farwell had asserted that he had been swindled by the New York Life agent, the notorious " Sam " Dinkelspiel, and had threatened suit. Such purchases were a fraud on the other policy-holders, as, according to the scheme, they were themselves entitled to the profits obtained from surrendered policies. Smaller holders did not receive such considerate treatment, and consequently many suits reached trial. The point especially aimed at was to gain access to the books, to ascertain the regularity with which they had been kept, the honesty with which the money received had been invested and disbursed. The policy-holders desired to learn the actual reasons for their small returns; whether they were explained by natural causes or extravagance and dishonesty in management. Naturally, the hostility manifested toward all investigations, legislative or judicial, impelled the desire for detailed information. The policy-holders therefore asserted that the companies were great holders of trust funds; that they had so completely failed to maintain their promises that general suspicion of improper methods existed; and that individual accounting to policy-holders must be made. The Equitable now repudiated the contention that it held policy-holders' premiums as a trustee. It interposed a demurrer in the case of Bewley against Equitable on these grounds: " The plaintiffs, as policy-holders, have no rights which entitle them to bring this action. The policy-holder is not *cestui que trust*. And neither the directors nor the company are trustees. The policy-holder is not a partner. He is not a creditor. He is not a member of the company. The fund produced by the payment of all the premiums does not in any sense belong to the policy-holders, but belongs exclusively to the company."

The courts generally have sustained this view. They have decided several times that the policy-holders' rights are purely contractual; and that such apportionment as the companies make must be accepted. Occasionally, however, a phrase in a decision aroused apprehension. Once or twice the Court of Appeals hinted that, in certain contingencies, an actual accounting might be obtained. Justice Peckham, in Frederick Ulman against the New York Life-Insurance Company, interjected a paragraph that caused general consternation in New York. Justice Peckham called attention to the fact that the policy contract called for an " equitable apportionment " of profits. Unless proofs to the contrary were submitted, the presumption that

an "equitable apportionment" had been made stood
in the company's favour. But, intimated Justice Peckham, should the policy-holders furnish proofs that an
inequitable apportionment had been made or that such
apportionment had been based upon "erroneous principles," then the court might with propriety open the
whole case. Hyde and his associates promptly met this
decision by practically shutting off their policy-holders
from access to the courts. They secured the passage
of the law which virtually prevented insurance companies from being sued. Under this law all suits for
an accounting must be brought, not by the policy-
holder himself, but by the *Attorney-General*. Probably
New York State never enacted a more infamous statute
than this; whether it is constitutional, has never been
judicially determined. It practically gave the insurance
companies a licence to loot the policy-holders at will.

"DEFERRED DIVIDEND," OR SEMI-TONTINE, SUCCEEDS THE TONTINE POLICY

Thus Hyde and his associates completed the several
links in a conspiracy that kept their policy-holders from
justice. In spite of this they had to abandon the Tontine game. The public, after nearly twenty years' trial,
finally grasped its meaning, and refused to purchase
full Tontine policies. Hyde at once invented another

new policy, similar to the old, but somewhat modified. About 1883 he announced another " great discovery " —his " semi-Tontine." In 1885 this became the " non-forfeiting " Tontine; in 1886 the " Free Tontine." This policy was practically identical with that now known as the " deferred dividend." It differed from the original Tontine in that it gave a surrender value on lapses. If you lapsed now, you did get a paid-up policy; you simply forfeited your " dividends." In the event of death before the Tontine period expired, you also forfeited all dividends. Unquestionably, the deferred dividend or semi-Tontine was a reform on the old idea, though in principle equally obnoxious. Hyde used the same methods of solicitation. His agents still canvassed by promising immense returns at the conclusion of the deferred dividend period. Hyde based his new estimates, however, upon " actual results." He took the " dividends " paid on full Tontines as estimates of probable payments upon semi-Tontines. If further evidence is required of the bad faith of all these estimates, this circumstance furnishes it. The " results " on full Tontines were made up largely out of lapsed policies; this great source of profit, as already said, did not exist in the case of the deferred dividend. How, then, could the results of semi-Tontines be expected to equal those on full Tontines? Of course, they never have.

Deferred dividend policy-holders have been just as
badly misled, just as keenly disappointed, as the
holders of the old Tontines.

Why have all the Tontine companies failed so mis-
erably to realise their early promises? It must be
granted that from the first the complete fufilment was
impossible. When 'pressed, the New York companies
have explained their failure chiefly on two grounds:
the fall in the interest rate, thus reducing expected
profits from investments; and the realisation of fewer
lapses than anticipated. Unquestionably, the interest
rate has fallen in thirty years; but the mathematicians have demonstrated that this accounts only to a
small degree for the Tontine deficits. Just how far the
failure to realise innumerable lapses explains the falling off we shall never know. Hyde always kept these
facts carefully concealed. The lapse rate under
Tontine, as already shown, was enormous. A third factor, which the New York companies have never brought
forth, better explains these small " dividends " than
a decreased interest rate and unrealised lapses. That
is an *increase in expenses*. On this point we have illu-
minating data. The Equitable's expense rate steadily

advanced under Tontine. In 1871, when the first Tontine Savings Fund policy was issued, the Equitable spent seventeen cents out of every dollar paid in as premiums, in expenses. In 1890, the year before the first twenty-year Tontine became due, it spent twenty-five.

An especially valuable authority on the subject is Mr. Theodore M. Banta, the present cashier of the New York Life. Mr. Banta has held influential offices in this company for nearly fifty years. He has witnessed the rise and the decline of the Tontine and the semi-Tontine scheme. In 1887 he presented a series of grave charges against the New York Life management. One of his severest counts was the Tontine system. He asserted that the management had become so extravagant that, had it not been for the increase in the market value of certain securities, the New York Life, at that moment, would have been insolvent. Referring to the " estimated results " made by certain experts, Mr. Banta declared that " the experts in question probably did not foresee that so large a share of the policy-holders' money would be squandered by extravagant business methods."

The Tontine and deferred dividend funds have been preyed upon and wasted chiefly in two ways: inside rings have personally profited from them, and greater sums have been wasted in the mad race for new business.

To make the whole process understandable we must revert once more to fundamental principles. Dividends or annual savings arise primarily from two sources. The company realises fewer death losses than those upon which it has based its premium prices, and a higher interest rate on its investments than it had assumed. The third element of possible savings is upon the loadings. These are the amounts added arbitrarily to the premiums to cover the cost of management. Obviously, the best managed companies are those that save the most from their loadings, get the largest returns from their investments consistent with safety, and so select their risks that they have the largest saving from mortality. In the main, the big New York companies have selected their insurance risks with care. Concerning certain branches of the New York Life's medical department—its South American and far eastern business—and its sub-standard risks—there may be considerable doubt; but all three do show a fair, though not remarkable, profit from mortality. The waste and dishonesty have affected chiefly those parts of the premiums which are supposed to provide for expenses and to be laid aside for investment.

ENORMOUS SALARIES GIVEN TO RELATIVES
AND FAVOURITES

Life-insurance expenses consist mainly of agency expenditures, administrative salaries, advertising, legal outlays, and taxes. Agency disbursements will be described in detail in the next chapter. Upon the salary list, millions which, under honest conditions, would have been returned to policy-holders as dividends, have been disbursed. This abuse dates back many years. Henry B. Hyde, from the very first, exacted heavy tribute. In the old times the officers regularly abstracted certain sums as secret " bonuses "; in three years the Mutual Life, as has been shown, thus appropriated $189,000, and charged it on the books as dividends paid to policy-holders. The New York Life, up to fifteen years ago, tolerated the same practice. William H. Beers, at the time he was deposed, drew $75,000 a year salary, and a bonus of $25,000. The New York companies have also multiplied offices in the most reckless fashion. The Equitable, in addition to a $100,000 president, had a $100,000 vice-president, three vice-presidents whose salaries ranged from $30,000 to $60,000 each, and secretaries, assistant secretaries, controllers, treasurers, and auditors almost without number. The New York Life had a $100,000 president, four vice-presidents receiving anywhere from $20,000 to $40,000, three second vice-presidents, each receiving from $18,000 to $30,000, and the usual assortment of secretaries, treasurers, controllers, auditors, and the rest. In many cases the directors multiplied these highly paid positions in order to find soft places for relatives and other hangers-on. John A. McCall makes his son, recently graduated from Harvard, secretary of the New York Life at $15,000 per annum; his son-in-law, vice-president at $35,000; another son-in-law, inspector of agencies at $15,000; a brother-in-law, auditor of the Paris office at $7500; a "boyhood friend," Andrew Hamilton, lobby generalissimo at heaven only knows what compensation. These large salaries explain to a greater degree than is commonly supposed the falling off in policy-holders' dividends. The Mutual paid in salaries to its home office more than $1,000,000 a year;[2] nearly half what its policy-holders received in dividends.

All these officers have shown the itching palm even in ludicrous details. They have taken everything that came their way, no matter how small. They have scrambled for elections to sub-committees, and to the boards and committees of subsidiary institutions, partly for the sake of directors' fees. They have frequently quieted

[2] It is fair to add that the Mutual, since these disclosures, has reduced its salary list by at least $330,000 a year.

protesting trustees by elections to committees, especially in the allied trust companies, where fees were large and frequent. Each attendant gets ten or twenty dollars; it was commonly remarked that, unless these dignified financiers were watched closely, they abstracted more than one gold eagle from the plate. On one historic occasion an especially grasping trustee was actually forced to disgorge an extra gold piece to which he had no legal claim. Almost invariably committeemen divided among those present the fees of the absentees. A year or so ago a high financial officer of the Mutual Life attended a committee meeting of a subsidiary trust company. It was purely technical; he was the only member present. He pocketed the whole $140 fees usually allotted to a full attendance. William H. Beers, while president of the New York Life, suddenly recalled one day that, by a strange oversight, he had not drawn any director's fees for the past twenty years. He at once had the cashier draw him a check for $2500 to square up the account. In 1904 the Equitable spent $44,000 in directors' fees. William H. McIntyre, in addition to a salary of $30,000, made $8640 annually in director's fees in the Equitable and its allied companies.

Under the head of legal expenses and advertising,
the companies have concealed enormous amounts spent
in corrupting legislatures and the press. The trustees
have thus purchased immunity for their own dishonesty
and delinquencies, and continued themselves in power.
Innocent persons never bribe and seldom pay blackmail;
but the managements of the New York companies have
done both for thirty-five years. In 1872, for example,
they collected $20,000 for legislative purposes; and the
particular favour sought in this instance is a fair indication of the motives that have usually prompted such
contributions. They sought the passage of a law which,
in effect, would have crushed their smaller rivals and
given them a monopoly. They have constantly used the
official machinery of the state against the interests of
their policy-holders. They have fought all liberalising
reforms. In the '70's they opposed, year after year,
bills providing surrender values on lapsed policies.
They have stood against all legislative attempts to prevent cheating by agents. They have opposed legislative
attacks on the Tontine and deferred dividend systems.
Their interests have become so diversified that they
have manifested interest in numerous questions not

immediately connected with insurance. They have kept watch of all legislation affecting banks, trust companies, safe deposit companies, railroads, and numerous other corporations. They have uniformly used their influence in such cases against the public good and in favour of privileged interests. They have amended the investment law twenty times in thirty years, not for the sake of protecting their policy-holders, but to permit investments along lines that guaranteed private profit to themselves. Above all, the insurance companies must control the legislature to prevent exposure. For thirty-five years have they stood on the brink of the *debacle* that has now arrived. In 1870 the insurance department investigated the Mutual. The Mutual, however, succeeded in stopping the proceedings just as they became interesting; and in suppressing the official records. In 1877 the Insurance Committee of the Senate took several hundred pages of testimony; but just as the relation between the Equitable and certain companies wrecked during the '70's was about to be unfolded, it suddenly adjourned and submitted no official report. Expenditures for these purposes, all at the cost of the policy-holders, date back many years. Henry B. Hyde, fifteen years before he died, began contributing to state campaign funds. Since 1896 the three big companies have given sums ranging from $25,000 to

$50,000 to the Republican National Committee. Hyde originated his famous " yellow dog " fund largely for legislative purposes. Mr. Hughes demonstrated that an alliance existed between the Equitable, the Mutual, and the New York Life for waging legislative warfare; that, however, is an old story. For many years Charlton T. Lewis managed the legislative campaign in their interest. Mr. Lewis was one of the most brilliant men of his time. He figured as a reformer in many lines, and was a classical scholar of recognised attainments. For nearly forty years, however, he used his splendid abilities in defending, in legislatures and out, the New York insurance companies.[4]

[4] As far back as September 18, 1878, Mr. Lewis wrote to the New York Life: " At a conference of the New York companies it was found that an addition to the subscription by the three largest companies of $900 by the New York Life and the Equitable (each) and $1350 by the Mutual will enable us to pay C. M. Depew, Esq., ($5000,) in addition to the obligations we have already assumed." In 1882 the three companies, also on requisition of Mr. Lewis, paid C. M. Depew $5000. In 1887, in connection with the repeal of a certain tax law, the New York Life paid Mr. Lewis $17,000: for " seven visits to Albany, $13,500, travelling expenses, $450, newspapers, $650, and three visits to Massachusetts, $2500." Mr. Lewis received the money in bills. Mr. Theodore M. Banta put the above voucher before the trustees of the New York Life in 1887, when the following colloquy took place:

Q. Who is Lewis?

A. (Banta) A lawyer in the Equitable Building. At one

The combination have paid the campaign expenses of senators and assemblymen in New York and other states; and have always controlled the insurance committees and dictated the appointment of insurance commissioners. Two insurance superintendents in New York State have been ejected from office for accepting their bribes. At the same time they have paid enormous sums in blackmail. They have patronised largely

time, years ago, there was a chamber of life insurance. It went out of existence. He was the controlling spirit in that. He is the party who is employed to look after legislatures.

Mr. Banta said that $100,000 was paid in 1887 by the three companies to Davies, Cole, and Rapallo for services in connection with the repeal of chapter 534 of the laws of 1880; of which the New York Life paid $17,241. He submitted a large number of vouchers showing the legislative activities of the combination extending back twenty years. Thus, under date of May 5, 1885, the following was addressed to the New York Life by the Equitable:

"Please send check to order of Henry B. Hyde for $1428.59 —legal services and disbursements for company's account"; and, December 29, 1885: "Please draw checks to order of Thomas Jordan, Cashier (of Equitable), for $7106.70 as below: Law expenses, $3968, Advertising, $1986.70, Miscellaneous, $1152." In 1886 the New York Life paid the following voucher: "J. W. Alexander, of the Equitable, check 34,330 sent to him 'personally' and not officially, $7402." Again the New York Life paid money to the Mutual, such vouchers as these being put in: "To H. J. Cullen, $7500, May 28, 1884. Note: Legal services and expenditures. This was given to Major Ulrich of the Mutual Life after Cullen had endorsed it and cashier had certified the endorsement so that currency could be drawn."

the twenty or thirty insurance papers that exist almost exclusively by so-called insurance " advertising." This, too, is an ancient abuse; we have already shown how the Mutual, in 1878, after imprisoning Stephen English, editor of the *Insurance Times*, for six months, finally bought him off for $35,000. Mr. Hughes recently revealed the fact that one Joe Howard, Jr., had drawn for several years $2500 from both the Mutual and the Equitable. By referring again to the trustees' investigation of the New York Life in 1887, we learn the antiquity of this custom and also get a capital insight into the nature of Howard's services. On the subject of " blackmail," Vice-President Archibald H. Welch testified as follows:

One day (in 1884) Howard sent in his card to me and presented a letter from President McCurdy of the Mutual Life. The letter was to this purport: "Mr. Howard has shown me some articles which have been brought to his notice. I feel it is a matter of interest to you, and therefore give this letter with suggestion that you give him careful attention." Howard opened up a large package of manuscript made up largely of severe attacks upon this company somewhat after the manner of those which had been largely published in some insurance journals. Some things which he had had not been published. He also had some matters which are contained in this charge. Insurance journals are read exclusively by insurance men. Howard stated that the documents were to be published in a leading New York paper and other papers. If those articles had been published, it would reach a large volume of outsiders that no statement we could make would reach, and if it did reach them it would not destroy the bad effect of the attack. Howard stated that he was the correspondent of several New York, Boston, and Washington papers. We considered it to the interest of the company that these things should not spread. I recognised the fact that this company is doing business largely on public confidence. We have that confidence, and to destroy or alarm it would be very disastrous to the interests of the company. There was no question in my mind but what it was best to suppress this article. The method of suppressing it we had to discuss. It was finally arranged that Howard should receive a certain specified sum—$5000.

We shall probably never know how much money has been spent in this fashion. That the New York Life has paid Andrew Hamilton $1,300,000 in the last ten years, for which he has rendered no accounting, has been proved; and unquestionably other disbursements have been so completely covered up that not a trace remains. The Mutual Life has wasted hundreds of thousands of dollars on its legislative agents which, in the official reports, have innocently figured as " stationery and supplies." To hide its tracks, it had forged the names of office boys, fixed up bogus vouchers, and paid bills to imaginary business houses created for this particular purpose. Its expenditures for advertising and supplies have aggregated, in one year, $1,134,000—half as much as it has paid in policyholders' dividends; that item, it is known, contains money spent on legislatures, blackmail, and in other illicit ways. Already two former vice-presidents have been indicted for perjury and forgery in connection with this account.

Hyde and his competitors also anticipated great Tontine and deferred dividend profits from excess interest earnings. At present the New York companies base their premiums upon three and three and one-half per cent. That they must earn to maintain solvency; anything beyond is theoretically returned to the policy-holders. Thus they have an absolute standard of investment earnings; the unpardonable sin is the realisation of less than three per cent. If they have securities yielding less than this minimum, they have a deficit in the reserves which must be made up from other sources—that is, the surplus. Because these companies have this great accumulation to fall back upon they have sunk millions in investments that do not realise the interest rate needed to maintain solvency. For at least twenty years the New York companies, to a great extent, have deliberately closed their eyes to the safest and most profitable investment opportunity—mortgage loans on New York real estate; and have placed their policy-holders' premiums in Wall

Street securities which return relatively a much lower rate. Thirty-five years ago the Equitable, the New York Life, and the Mutual invested more than sixty per cent. of their funds in mortgage loans; now they have only about fifteen. The New York Life sins most grievously. It has total assets amounting to $390,-000,000; and only $23,000,000, or less than six per cent., invested in first mortgages. Both the Mutual Benefit and the Northwestern, on the other hand, have more than fifty per cent. of their assets thus put away. First mortgages are especially valuable assets for life-insurance companies. When made with honesty and judgment, they combine safety with liberal returns. Moreover, the insurance company, unlike the national bank, does not need " quick assets." It is not subject to " runs." Its contracts mature regularly; and it knows years in advance what its cash obligations will be. For five years preceding the present upheaval the New York Life practically refused even to entertain applications for mortgage loans. Instead, it established a branch office in the heart of Wall Street, placed in charge Mr. George W. Perkins, a member of the firm of J. Pierpont Morgan & Company, and invested exclusively in stock-market securities.

These managements do not like mortgage loans, simply because they do not afford opportunities for personal advancement and reward. They cannot manipulate them; they cannot buy and sell them at will; there is " nothing in it " for themselves. In saying this we need not necessarily imply that trustees directly profit by the sale and purchase of these securities—though that has happened. The impelling motive is more deep-seated. If they invest in realty loans, they remove themselves from associations with the great men of the time. They do not associate with great bankers, railroad owners, captains of industry. They will not obtain appointments to the boards of great corporations; have their names put down for syndicate participations; be taken in, when great enterprises are floated, on the ground floor, nor obtain tips on the stock market. For example, Mr. James H. Hyde held directorship in some fifty corporations, largely traceable to investments held by the Equitable Life. All investments are made by finance committees; the members of these finance committees invariably hold directorships in endless banks, trust companies, railroads, and miscellaneous corporations. They get these positions, and the enormous opportunities for personal profit furnished thereby, simply by virtue of the investments they make for their insurance companies. In other words, to advance themselves they sacrifice millions in interest earnings for their policy-holders. Of forty-

five leading life-insurance companies, the Equitable
Life has realised the smallest investment returns. Close
competitors for this position are the Mutual and the
New York Life.

DIVIDENDS EATEN UP BY DEPRECIATING OFFICE BUILDINGS

Instead of buying first mortgage liens, the New
York companies have preferred investments directly
in fee property. They have had a mania for enormous
office buildings. Three together, in the last thirty-five
years, have put not less than $100,000,000 into prop-
erty of this kind. Henry B. Hyde originated this reform. He erected the first Equitable building largely
for the purpose of display, as an outward manifestation of the Society's greatness and stability. He believed that the average American would rather insure
in a company dwelling in a splendid monument of this
sort than in one with unpretentious headquarters. As
soon as he had finished the first Equitable building, he
therefore put up a counterpart in Boston. Others followed in Philadelphia, Chicago, and other large cities
of the West. He also erected monuments to the Equitable in Paris, Berlin, Madrid, Vienna, Melbourne, Syd-
ney, and other foreign places. The New York Life and
the Mutual have followed his example. The New York

Life has buildings in Belgrade, Budapest, and Amsterdam; the Mutual has one at Cape Town.

On these buildings the policy-holders have lost in a variety of ways. In the first place the buildings have, as a rule, tremendously depreciated in value. The total cost of the present Equitable building in New York was $18,000,000. Its present value, on the Equitable's own estimate, is not more than $15,000,000. Only the phenomenal growth in Broadway land values has saved the policy-holders from a much greater loss. The New York Life's Broadway building cost $7,121,000; the company now claims a valuation of only $5,000,000. The Mutual's main office building in New York cost $17,277,000; the Mutual has written off more than $6,000,000 in the last seven years. Many of the foreign buildings show similar depreciations. The Equitable's 'Melbourne " advertisement " cost $2,864,000; the Society at present gives it a value of only $2,000,000. The first New York Life building in Paris cost $1,102,-000; in 1891 the French government valued it at $470,000. The present Paris building cost $2,500,000; the company now gives it a value of $1,300,000. The Equitable has invested $37,884,000 in its fifteen office buildings; the insurance department in order to give them an earning power of three per cent. has placed the value at $26,000,000—a loss of $11,500,000.

Should the properties actually be sold, the depreciation would probably be even larger.

But the policy-holders have lost not only in capital value. For years many of these buildings have earned much less than the interest rate upon which the companies have based their premiums. In 1887 Theodore M. Banta declared that the New York Life's Broadway building did not earn enough to pay taxes and the cost of keeping it clean. One of the most serious charges brought against President Beers was the loss on this structure. John A. McCall had hardly taken office, however, when he started a building several times larger than the old one. On this the New York Life realises about two and one-half per cent. Its Minneapolis building pays two and one-half; those at Montreal and St. Paul only about one. The Equitable, after reducing its building valuations from $37,000,000 to $31,000,000, was still unable to earn, on the majority, the interest rate on which it had based its premiums. On nine of them it earns anywhere from 1.56 to 2.98 per cent. Let us trace the history of one of these structures, showing precisely how the policy-holders have suffered. The Equitable erected the Boston building in the '70's at a cost of $2,342,979.73. It then calculated its premiums at four per cent. That is, the income from this structure should be some $93,700.

In fact it earns only about $23,000. Here is an annual loss of $71,400 on this one piece of real estate, an amount which must be obtained elsewhere to make solvent that particular asset. It comes out of the surplus—upon the money that is laid aside for "dividend" purposes. Properly invested, that $2,342,000 should yield more than four per cent., and thus contribute some surplus itself. But, far from increasing policy-holders' dividends, it decreases them. In fact, these office buildings have constantly prevented policy-holders from receiving the benefit of other investments more advantageously made. The Mutual Life, and to a less extent the New York Life, have frequently realised good profits from the sale of general securities. Such profits, which otherwise would have been returned as "dividends," have been used instead to wipe out losses on real estate. From 1895 to 1905, for example, the Mutual sold securities for $12,786,000 more than it paid for them. That handsome profit ought to have benefited the policy-holders. But $9,000,000 was used to reduce valuations on real estate, and thus bring it to a better percentage showing. In twenty-five years the Equitable has wasted some $30,000,000 in real estate alone—money which, under proper management, would have been paid to policy-holders in dividends.

WHY THE OFFICE BUILDINGS HAVE NOT PAID

The policy-holders have not realised profits upon
these buildings largely because they have been managed dishonestly. Henry B. Hyde first showed how to
use them for private profit; and his competitors have
proved apt pupils. He charged the Equitable Society
itself an enormous rental for space occupied in its own
building; but foisted upon it, at absurdly low prices
as tenants, favoured persons and corporations in which
he had a personal interest. In the early '70's he founded
the Mercantile Safe Deposit Company, owning the majority of the stock himself. The Equitable Society
obligingly fitted up special quarters for this in its
own building, and installed an expensive plant of safe
deposit boxes and vaults. The Equitable, for the last
fifteen years, has received net rentals for this establish-
ment amounting to $230 per annum—not enough to pay
for maintenance, light, heat, and janitor services. The
Hyde family and their associates, however, have received in the neighbourhood of $87,000 a year. The
Equitable Society, that is, furnishes the entire plant,
rent, and largely the maintenance; the Hyde interests
take all the profit. This arrangement continues until
the year 2001, when the lease, with its renewals, expires.
Hyde himself also rented, on similar terms, choice

quarters in the Boston building for safe deposit purposes. In this case the Equitable has not only obtained
no rent, but has expended thousands of dollars for the
benefit of the Safe Deposit Company. The Hyde family
and their associates, however, net some $36,000 a year.
This arrangement will expire about two centuries
hence. Hyde also rented himself spacious quarters in
the Equitable's St. Louis building—again for safe
deposit purposes—paying therefor $100 per annum.
Henry G. Marquand, famous as a patron of art and
a donor of private chapels to theological seminaries,
was Hyde's most conspicuous partner in this Missouri
enterprise. For years the directors and many officers
of the Equitable knew nothing of these leases. They
were not kept among the Equitable's official papers.
Superintendent Hendricks finally discovered them in
the personal possession of William H. McIntyre, for
years Henry B. Hyde's confidential man.

About 1885 the New York Life followed in Hyde's
footsteps. It leased the basement in its Broadway building to the Manhattan Safe Deposit Company for $12,-
000 a year, although a well-known dry-goods firm had
offered it $22,000 for the same quarters. The Manhat-
tan Safe Deposit Company consisted of the New York
Life and its high officers and trustees. But this business
did not go well; the Manhattan Safe Deposit Company

got deeply into debt. When failure became inevitable, the New York Life purchased, at par, the stock with which its own trustees found themselves encumbered. The policy-holders, that is, kindly relieved their own trustees of a very bad investment. In the Mutual Life Building there are also safe deposit companies, in which Mutual directors hold office and stock; but full details concerning these have not yet been obtained.

FIFTY TRUST COMPANIES AND BANKS FEEDING ON THE POLICY-HOLDERS

Henry B. Hyde also originated the subsidiary trust company. Back in 1870 he organised the Mercantile Trust Company, and installed it in the Equitable Building. Later he added to the Equitable the American Deposit & Loan Company, the Western National Bank, and large interests in some fifty other financial institutions. In 1888 the New York Life organised, for similar purposes, the New York Security & Trust Company; in 1892 the Mutual started the United States Mortgage & Trust Company. Together, the three now own largely in nearly fifty allied financial institutions. They have kept on deposit in them not far from $75,000,000, always at low interest rates, usually two per cent. We need only recall again the fundamental investment conditions under which life

companies operate to detect the fraud. The New York
companies must earn at least three per cent. to maintain solvency; under present investment conditions
they can readily get four and one-half; and yet they
have placed in these allied institutions nearly $75,000,-
000 at about two per cent.[5] The policy-holders annually lose nearly $2,000,000 in this way. For these
balances there is no legitimate justification. Insurance
companies need not carry large bank balances in order
to provide against heavy and unexpected calls. The
Equitable has a regular weekly cash income of $1,500,-
000; its weekly expenditures are less than $1,000,000.
Neither do they need large balances as a basis for
demanding loans and other banking accommodations;
they themselves have more available cash than they
can use, and should look for opportunities to lend,
not borrow. Better managed life companies do not
carry such great balances. The Northwestern Mutual,
for example, has had for several years less than two
per cent. of its assets in bank, whereas the Equitable
has had more than nine. But in all cases the New York
companies are large holders of stock in the favoured
depositories. Invariably, prominent trustees, usually
members of the finance committees, personally hold

[5] Since the recent disclosures the New York companies have
materially reduced these bank balances.

stock, and, as trustees of the subsidiary concerns, practically direct their affairs. In many cases they left this money with the distinct promise that they would not draw against it. In 1903, for example, President Alexander, in a letter to Vice-President Hyde, described the Equitable as "strapped for money by engagements already made," and declared that he was straining every nerve to raise $1,000,000 by a specified date. At that time the Equitable had bank balances of $37,000,000, nominally subject to check. The New York Life for several years carried anywhere from $3,000,000 to $13,000,000 with the New York Security & Trust Company, in which the company and nearly all the leading trustees held stock. The Mutual Life left for years flat sums ranging from $250,000 to $8,500,000 with from fifteen to twenty banks and trust companies, in practically all of which the company and the directors personally owned shares.

In other words, the New York companies have furnished working capital, at low rates of interest, to some fifty allied institutions. These institutions lend this money out at a profit, and use it in other money-making ways. New York Life officers admitted that they left from $3,000,000 to $13,000,000 with the New York Security & Trust Company, that it might have an available capital upon which it could rely in making loans. Whenever the trust company had a good opportunity to make large loans, the New York Life increased its deposit for that particular purpose. In return, the trust company paid the New York Life one-half of one per cent. less than it obtained itself; in other words, it made one-half of one per cent. out of millions that belonged to the policy-holders. Mr. McCurdy, Mr. Hyde, and Mr. McCall attempted to justify this practice on the ground that their insurance companies, as large stock-holders themselves in the trust companies, obtained profits in the shape of dividends, and also in the increase in the value of their stock. Both these arguments are inadmissible. Every investment must stand on its own merits; large profits on trust company's stocks do not justify large losses on trust company deposits. Moreover, even allowing for the dividends received, the companies have not found their trust company affiliations profitable. The Mutual's net return, after deducting its loss on deposits from its profits as dividends, is little more than three per cent.; the Equitable's, little more than one. Again, the increase in the value of the stocks cannot be admitted as an asset. The quotations of the trust company stocks depend largely upon insurance affiliations and deposits; withdraw these, and the value is problematical.

POLICY-HOLDERS' PROFITS TRANSFERRED TO ALLIED
TRUST COMPANIES

In other ways the trust companies prey on the
policy-holders. The Mutual Life, for example, purchases the debentures of the United Sates Mortgage
& Trust Company. This latter corporation invests
largely in Western mortgages. It obtains from four,
four and one-half to five per cent., and sells these—or
debenture certificates based upon them—to the Mutual
Life at four. In other words, it takes the policy-
holders' money, invests it at four and one-half per
cent., and pays the policy-holders four—thus making
from one-half to one and one-half per cent. itself.
The Mutual Life could make all these loans directly;
the Northwestern Mutual and the Union Central hold
similar securities in large amounts, but do it without
such expensive intermediaries. The Mutual has invested $6,000,000 in this way. Both the Mutual and
the Equitable buy mortgages on similar terms from
the Title Guarantee & Trust Company, of New York,
and the Lawyers' Mortgage Company. Notwithstanding the fact that they have their own machinery for
lending on New York City real estate, they prefer
to give the profit to companies in which Hyde, Mc-
Curdy, *et al.* have pecuniary interests. The Equitable

has in other ingenious ways fleeced its policy-holders
through the trust companies. In 1905, for example, it
had advanced not far from $7,000,000 to its agents
against future commissions. Since 1894 the insurance
departments have refused to admit these as valid assets.
The ingenious Henry B. Hyde then adopted the plan
of assigning these loans to the Commercial Trust Company, of Philadelphia. Virtually—though this was not
the precise form of the transaction—he deposited the
money in the trust company at three per cent. interest.
The trust company lent it to his agents at five. That
is, its stockholders make a two per cent. profit on this
large sum.

INSURANCE COMPANIES BENEVOLENT "GRAND-MOTHERS"

Life-insurance trustees have also diverted to their
trust companies profits that belonged to policy-holders.
They have used the latter's credit in underwriting syndicates, and then given part of the profits to these
allied institutions. Trustees have obtained favours in
the shape of loans. They have borrowed large sums in
the names of their stenographers, frequently on insuf-
ficient collateral; and have let the loans run for years,
sometimes not even paying interest promptly. Through
the trust companies they have used the policy-holders'

money in speculative enterprises. If the thing went well, the trust company kept the profits; if ill, it was sometimes turned over to the parent insurance company. Indeed, the officers of the United States Mortgage & Trust Company commonly referred to the Mutual Life as their " grandmother." If a speculative enterprise turned out badly, the " old lady " sometimes relieved them of it. In 1899, for example, the United States Mortgage & Trust Company reorganised the Washington Traction & Electric Company. The public refused to invest, and the trust company found itself inconveniently loaded up with $1,000,000 unsalable bonds. The " old lady " obligingly purchased these, although it already had $2,000,000 which it had taken as the result of a syndicate participation. In 1894 Henry B. Hyde discovered that the Western National Bank, in which he and the Equitable owned stock, was practically insolvent. It had reached this condition by lending $600,000 on a wildcat land scheme in Kentucky. Mr. Hyde quietly transferred this collateral to the Mercantile Trust Company, paying the Western National Bank cash. Later he spent through the trust company enormous sums in a useless attempt to make the collateral valuable. After his death James W. Alexander had the whole obligation, amounting to $2,600,000, transferred to the policy-

holders of the Equitable Society.*   The New York Security & Trust Company has also found a benevolent
" grandmother " in the New York Life. It also reorganised a street electric system, this time in New
Orleans. After the reorganisation the company went
into a receiver's hands, and the New York Security &
Trust Company had some $3,800,000 in unsalable se-
curities. The New York Life kindly relieved it of the
burden; and afterward sold the bonds at a loss of
$326,000 to the policy-holders.

PROFITS FROM SPECULATIVE SYNDICATES

Trustees have also plundered the policy-holders by
the purchase and sale of securities and through engagements in speculative enterprises, such as syndicates and joint accounts.

In the Equitable the syndicate dates back many
years. Records of eighteen exist in Henry B. Hyde's
time. In its only legitimate form, the syndicate is a
combination of investors, personal and corporate, for
the actual purchase of securities.   It is thus only another manifestation of the magnitude of modern business enterprise. A great railroad, for example, offers
$50,000,000 in bonds in a single issue. Manifestly, few

* It is fair to add that the present management of the Equitable has repudiated this obligation.

bankers are strong enough to assume such a large flotation without promises of support. The banking house, therefore, forms a syndicate among certain investors, each agreeing to take a certain proportion at a specified price. Among the largest investors are the three big New York insurance companies. If they actually take the bonds at the price at which they have subscribed, and place them away in their vaults for investment, the operation is entirely free from criticism. But that is precisely what they have not done. Indeed, according to modern Wall Street ethics, the purchase of syndicate securities at the original subscription price is regarded as distinctly bad form. The presidents and treasurers plaintively declared that had they thus mortally offended the bankers, they would have received no more participations. They are expected to buy these securities, not at the price at which they have subscribed, but at one higher.

The members of underwriting syndicates are not primarily customers. They are guarantors. They put down their names for certain allotments merely to assure the success of the flotation. The bankers pledge themselves to sell the securities, if possible, in the general market. Only in the event that it does not take them, do the syndicate members actually buy. Speyer & Company, for example, purchase from the Republic of Cuba $35,000,000 worth of bonds at eighty-nine. In order to safeguard themselves, Speyer & Company form a syndicate, the members of which agree to purchase at that price. With this assurance, Speyer & Company can continue the operation in complete safety to themselves, for they have an assured sale. However, they have no intention of selling directly to the syndicate members. They dispose of the whole allotment to the general public at prices varying from ninety-one to ninety-seven. The difference between the eighty-nine at which the syndicate subscribed and the price at which the general public purchases is profit. This, Speyer & Company divide among the members of the syndicate. It is their compensation for the guarantee. They have theoretically assumed a considerable risk; that is, had the public not taken the bonds, the syndicate would have had to, and realised a loss. This has actually happened. J. P. Morgan & Company, for example, three years ago formed an underwriting syndicate to guarantee $50,000,000 International Mercantile Marine bonds. The public did not buy; and many disgruntled participators, including the New York Life and the Mutual, have large blocks of these unsalable securities on hand. Essentially, in other words, syndicates are purely speculative.

Trustees of life-insurance companies, who have thus speculated, have enjoyed unusual advantages. Their syndicate speculations have usually turned out fortunately. That is because they have had at hand large purchasers of securities—*i. e.*, their own life-insurance companies. Their syndicate gamblings have been most unsportsmanlike, for they have bet upon " sure things." The syndicate managers always expect that the companies will purchase largely in the market; and that is the reason they have let the insurance magnates in. They have always placed these opportunities for profit where they would do the most good. In the Equitable they have selected James H. Hyde, James W. Alexander, Chauncey M. Depew, William H. McIntyre, and other members of the finance committee; in the Mutual, Richard A. McCurdy, Robert A. Grannis, Frederic Cromwell, George G. Haven, A. D. Juillard, and others similarly high-placed. These gentlemen, as participtors in syndicates, made profits contributed, to a considerable extent, by the purchases which they made for their own insurance companies. Take that very case of the Cuban bonds. They all subscribed at eighty-nine; but the Mutual Life purchased its bonds in the open market at ninety-two. The directors salved their consciences by admitting the Mutual Life itself into the syndicate as a participator in the profits. The Mutual, that is, usually played two rôles: as a member of the syndicate and as part of the " general public " which purchased the securities. The Equitable did not usually observe such niceties. Years ago Henry B. Hyde formed his own syndicates, purchased securities at ground-floor prices, and sold them to the Equitable at generous profits. He called his syndicates " Louis Fitzgerald and Associates," and " George H. Squire and Associates." His son, following the parental example, named his " James H. Hyde and Associates." In some cases he gave the Equitable itself a share of the swag; more frequently he did not. In 1902 James H. Hyde formally notified Kuhn, Loeb & Company in future to put all participations usually assigned the Equitable in his own name; his object in this was to get the profits himself instead of giving them to the policy-holders. Let us trace a few of these operations. On June 11, 1902, " James H. Hyde and Associates " subscribed to $1,000,000 Metropolitan Street Railway bonds at ninety-four; seven days later they sold the same to the Equitable at ninety-seven and one-half—pocketing profits of $30,000 without risking a dollar of their own. On October 28 they obtained $1,250,000 Oregon short line bonds at ninety-six; five days later they sold them to the Equitable at ninety-seven. Mr. Hyde and Mr. Alexander made

$25,044 by this deal. Occasionally syndicate managers required working capital, and then issued " calls " to the members. Frequently they needed this only temporarily, and returned it after concluding the transaction. In such cases the " old lady " supplied the cash. Thus, in 1901, J. P. Morgan & Company allotted the Equitable Society a $1,500,000 participation in Chicago, Burlington & Quincy bonds. The Equitable itself, however, got only $500,000; James H. Hyde, James W. Alexander, Louis Fitzgerald, Chauncey M. Depew, and other members of the finance committee took the lion's share themselves. When a " call " for cash was made, however, the Equitable paid not only its own proportion, but that of these philanthropic trustees. Later, the Equitable purchased all the bonds at a price much in excess of that paid by the syndicate. In this transaction, in which the Equitable had supplied all the cash, it realised in profits $7729; and Messrs. Hyde, Alexander, Depew, and the rest, for which they had not risked a single dollar, some $28,000. The trustees exclaim that the policy-holders have lost nothing; that they have good bonds, usually worth more than they have paid for them. But they have lost. That their own trustees might profit, they have paid excessive prices for their investments. In some cases they have received bad securities: the old Henry B. Hyde syndicates frequently forced undersirable bonds upon the Society.

Why the Mutual, the Equitable, and the New York Life make relatively the poorest showing on investments of some forty American life companies must now be sufficiently apparent. Why they have generally failed to make good their agents' " estimates " of profits is also partly explained. The greatest source of extravagance and waste, however—the millions spent in the solicitation of new business, the mania for size—still remains to be described.

CHAPTER VII

THE RACE FOR BIGNESS

THE policy-holders have suffered most, not from the dishonesty of their trustees, but from their recklessness and extravagance. The amounts abstracted by underwriting syndicates and high salaries are insignificant compared with the millions wasted upon the agents. The overshadowing evil has been the craze for size. In the last thirty years the Mutual, the Equitable, and the New York Life have concentrated their energies upon a single end. They have aimed at leadership, not in providing the safest and fairest and lowest-cost life insurance, but in writing the largest annual new business. They have aimed at quantity, not quality. They have become the most conspicuous illustration of the American passion for bigness. They have thus Barnumized the business. To this one fact the larger evils are directly traced.

These evils, outside of the actual dishonesty of the trustees, are the high cost of life insurance and its frequently deceptive and fraudulent character. The high cost is explained by outrageous payments to agents, in the shape of commissions, prizes, bonuses, and miscellaneous forms of entertainment; by reckless advertising, rebates, and advances; and by the solicitation of business in foreign countries at the expense of the American members. Such expenditures, like most other details, are theoretically graded on a mathematical basis. Every policy-holder, as already explained, pays a certain " loading " on his premium each year as his contribution to management expenses. At age forty, for example, a $10,000 policy in the Equitable costs $330 a year. Of that, about $247 represents the actual cost of the insurance; and $82 the policy-holder's assessment for management expenses. Theoretically, the company expends as little of this loading as possible, and returns its savings in the shape of dividends—in other words, reduces, by that much, the cost of insurance. The connection between expenditures and the cost of life insurance thus clearly appears. The company which manages its agency system with the greatest economy and thus makes the largest savings from " loadings " will return the largest dividends, or furnish insurance at the lowest cost. How grievously the New York companies have sinned a few statistics will show. The New York Life, in 1903, spent $11,406,482 on the new business obtained that year, It collected in new premiums $13,-

784,000. In 1904 it spent $12,005,090 on new business; it collected in new premiums $13,988,186. The Equitable and the Mutual make a showing equally bad or worse. These three companies, that is, have much exceeded their entire loadings [1] in management expenses —notwithstanding the fact that their loadings are outrageously large. In other words, these companies have annually paid to agents, on new business, nearly ninety cents out of every dollar taken in. In many instances they have greatly overstepped this record. The Equitable, for example, has obtained its large English business by paying $1.25 for every dollar received in new premiums. In Australia it has paid out $1.40 for every dollar taken in.

"DEFERRED DIVIDENDS" WASTED ON AGENTS

The conservative business man stands aghast at such extravagance. He cannot understand how such methods have not ended, long ago, in bankruptcy. The explanation, however, is found in the one word

[1] The Equitable, according to its annual reports, has not exceeded its loading. Inasmuch as it has for years regularly concealed one of its greatest expenditures, "advances to agents," by transferring them to subsidiary trust companies, the exact facts are not ascertained. In the last eight months all three companies have shown some retrenchment in the cost of new business.

" Tontine." The companies have maintained perfect solvency in the face of such pressure because they have largely used the withheld dividends of their policy-holders. They have persuaded the public, by false and unfulfilled promises of enormous rewards, to leave their dividends for varying periods, usually twenty years. They have then largely used them in the hunt for new business. Many of their foreign establishments, had they been independent companies, would have become insolvent years ago. The New York managers, however, have made up the deficits by using the withheld " dividends " of the American members. The New York Life has confessed that, for agents' commissions and other acquisition expenses, it " borrowed," in the years 1903 and 1904, some $13,000,000 of policy-holders' dividends. Richard A. McCurdy has admitted, on the witness-stand, that the Mutual has similarly eaten into sacred trust funds, and has justified himself on the " missionary " principle. It was wiser, he declared, to use dividends in extending the business than in paying them to policy-holders, who, at best, would spend them foolishly.

New business is desirable, but not essential. A solvent company can stop now, never write another policy, pay off all its claims as they mature, and quietly cease to exist. The Equitable could shut its doors on new

policy-holders to-day and carry out its contracts to
the end. True, it would take nearly a hundred years
to do it; but every solvent company, thanks to Elizur
Wright's legal reserve law, is thus fortunately situ-
ated. A life company exists, however, for the purpose of insuring lives; and, for this reason alone, it
necessarily solicits new members. The extent to which
such new members may be admitted, like all life-insurance principles, is scientifically ascertained. A certain
membership is required to maintain a fair average of
mortality. The more lives insured, up to a certain
point, the more accurately will the mortality tables
upon which the premiums are based work in practice.
A company with one hundred lives could not succeed,
because all might conceivably die in one year, instead
of in the gradual succession anticipated by the mortality table. A company with ten thousand well-selected
lives or more, however, need expect no surprises. The
big New York companies have more than half a
million each, an excess which, merely from the ground-
work of mortality average, adds nothing to their
strength. They could split themselves into twenty or
thirty smaller companies, each as strong and solvent
as the parent concern. The other rational reason for
an increased size is a logical decrease in management
expenses. Obviously, the more policy-holders contribute

to the cost of running the company, the smaller should
be each one's share of the fixed charges. As long as
an increasing business decreases expenses, it is an ex-
cellent thing. Quite the contrary has happened, however. The New York companies' increasing business
has resulted in an increased expenditure. The new
members, that is, have not paid their own way, but
have become a burden upon the old policy-holders.
Life insurance is about the only modern enterprise
in which competition has increased the cost of the
product.

The desire for new business, obtained at this cost,
is explained first by the ambition of the particular
men in charge. Henry B. Hyde's enthusiasm, as has
already been said, was to found " not the best but the
biggest life-insurance company in the world." He set
the pace which the others felt impelled to follow. The
pride of the particular company and the ambition of
the men in charge were at stake. To a considerable
extent we can sympathise with these officers. In the
early '80's it was generally believed that the Mutual
Life was on the down grade, simply because its new
business, compared with that of its two great rivals,
showed a marked falling off. In fact, it was a far
better company than either; and, in giving way to the
modern manias, steadily deteriorated to their level. In

1891 John A. McCall took charge of the New York Life. Had Mr. McCall attempted to reform conditions and refused to write new business at the expense of the old policy-holders, unquestionably he would have been looked upon as a failure and ejected from office. Jacob L. Greene, who had sufficient force of character to champion and practise reform, was always regarded, by hustling life-insurance men, as a "back number." Unquestionably, the craze for bigness has a more corrupt explanation. The officers have based their demands for high and enormous salaries on their companies' increase in size. Their own importance has vastly grown as their companies' assets have piled up. A man with $400,000,000 or $500,000,000 under his control, with an annual income of $60,000,000 requiring investment, has become a financial giant. Few magnates have been so courted and flattered; few, under a constant pressure of flattery, have become so tyrannical. James H. Hyde, a year or two after leaving Harvard, sent a gorgeously framed picture of himself to the president of one of the largest New York financial houses, with a request that he hang it over his desk. It represented the young man in evening dress, with the pompadour hair, the violets, and all the other now celebrated regalia. The president in question submissively acceded.

Insurance leaders have thus obtained numerous chances to grow rich—and not necessarily at their policy-holders' direct expense. Again, there has developed a great administrative machine dependent upon this enormous new business for existence. If their companies refuse to accept this new business, thousands of agents must lose employment. If they cut commission rates, these agents would also support themselves with difficulty. And, be it remembered, the officers were at their agents' mercy. The agents, in the Mutual and the New York Life, delivered the votes, or proxies, that kept the trustees in power. Manifestly, the larger and more scattered the companies, the more securely they entrenched themselves. A mutual company with 1000 policy-holders located in the same community could readily combine to put out unfaithful trustees; one with 600,000 or 700,000 scattered all over five continents could do so only with the utmost difficulty. Thus has developed a series of motives, none of them in the policy-holder's interest, but distinctly opposed to it, all demanding a constantly increasing business, and all inspiring the management to the most reckless and dishonest methods of obtaining it.

LIFE-INSURANCE AGENTS NECESSARY

Theoretically, no life-insurance company should employ an agency force. He who has dependents and no income except the product of his own toil is as morally bound to carry life insurance as he is to furnish his children food and shelter. Obviously, he should not be hounded into performing this simple duty. However, that theory seldom works. Experience has demonstrated that men do not insure of their own free will. They must be clubbed into it. The company that employs no agents does no business. The old Equitable of London pays enormous " bonuses " or " dividends "; which means that it furnishes insurance at very low cost. However, it writes only a few hundred policies a year, and, at the present rate, must eventually cease to exist. Both circumstances—its big dividends and its small amount of new business—have the same explanation: the old Equitable has no agents. If you wish a policy you voluntarily buy it over the counter. Consequently, the New York companies, which do employ agents, have entered England and practically driven this old institution out of business. There is also a powerful actuarial justification for the agency system. Properly regulated, it brings only healthy lives into the company. A man anticipating early death does not

need to be persuaded; he is only too glad to obtain a
policy. That is the class which voluntarily seeks insurance. Indeed, an unsolicited applicant is always
regarded with suspicion and subjected to an unusually
rigid medical examination. Life-insurance agents, if
kept within restraint, perform an indispensable function in the social order. Few men are more ridiculed
and maltreated; few, after all, actually accomplish
more good. We are annoyed beyond measure at their
persistence; but that very persistence has provided
millions of helpless women and children with support.
The widow who receives the life company's check, after
the death of her protector, takes an entirely different
view of the insurance agent's importunities from that
taken by the husband who had to be hounded into a
policy.

Under modern pressure, however, the New York
companies have combed every social and professional
class in the search for solicitors. Each, in this country
alone, has from 10,000 to 15,000 men. In New York
City there are 5000 life-insurance agents. Apparently,
no citizen exists, in the companies' estimation, who does
not possess abilities in this direction. They employ men
and women, educated and ignorant, high and low born.
Broken-down clergymen, superannuated college pro-
fessors, briefless lawyers, bankrupt business men, cast-

off politicians, actors, reporters, artists—they press all into service. Evidently the managers argue that every man has a few friends, and is useful at least until he has exhausted them. "Anyone who has two hands and a hip pocket for a rate book can become an agent," —so say life-insurance men themselves. The New York companies make a special bid for conspicuous persons. They have colonels and generals in plenty; even ex-governors and congressmen. In addition to regular solicitors, who give up all their time to the work, they have emissaries who solicit in connection with other occupations. There is hardly a tenement house on the East Side of New York in which the Big Three have not each a representative. In every factory and every sweatshop have deferred dividends been sold. Bakers, grocers, butchers, and fish-cart peddlers have done an insurance business on the quiet. Of the 5000 employees of one of New York's largest clothing establishments at least 1500, it is said, have carried rate books.

A matron of a leading New York hospital was once discovered soliciting life insurance. One of the Big Three, a few years ago, planned to make every barber in Greater New York a solicitor. The barber enjoys exceptional opportunities for conversation, and, it was thought, could utilise these better in booming a particular life-insurance company than in indulging in the usual frivolities. The New York companies have originated what is practically a secret service system. They have what are known to the profession as " boosters," or " helpers,"—men at low salaries, who blaze the way for the real solicitor. The " boosters " hunt up possible policy-holders, get all the essential facts concerning their financial standing and physical condition, and then turn them over to the regular men. An intricate system of espionage has also developed. The Big Three have employed " spotters " or " stool-pigeons " to keep them informed, especially on big risks. Bank clerks, apartment-house janitors, elevator men have " tipped them off " concerning the doings of opposing companies. If you are solicited for a policy of any size by the Mutual, their rivals at once learn of it, and get hot on your trail. Probably some confidential clerk, for a few dollars, has started them on your scent.

AN OPENING FOR COLLEGE GRADUATES

A few years ago the Equitable began proselyting among the colleges. Its president visited New Haven, Cambridge, and other university towns, lecturing learnedly on " life insurance as a profession." It started at the same time its celebrated " summer school " in the Equitable library. On the nomination of several college presidents, some three or four hundred young bachelors of arts were gravely instructed how to sell Tontine policies and gold bonds by certain adepts in the Equitable's employ. The most popular lecturer was the venerable Archibald C. Haynes, who, after borrowing some $850,000 of policy-holders' money, was recently dismissed by President Morton. These university students were given liberal allowances while learning the trade, and then let loose on society. There are only a few now in the Equitable's employ.

For the last thirty years the Big Three have also largely recruited from each other's staffs. How Henry B. Hyde bought off his rival's most successful men has already been described. Indeed, the main rivalry has waged, not over the solicitation of new buisness, but the solicitation of agents. The New York companies have reasoned that they could sell any amount and any form of insurance if they only obtained sufficiently skilful men. As soon as a successful producer appeared in the Equitable's ranks, the Mutual and the New York Life at once began to tempt him away. They would offer higher commissions, guarantees, and salaries, and frequently actual initial bonuses. Companies less lenient with their policy-holders' dividends have had the utmost difficulty in building up agencies.

Twenty-five years ago Mr. John I. D. Bristol began organising a Northwestern Mutual agency in New York. The Big Three, first of all, attempted to pur- chase him, and, failing in that, assailed him in every possible way. Mr. Bristol practically ran a training- school for his three big rivals. He would spend several months painfully developing a good agent, and then Mc- Curdy, Beers, or Hyde would at once add him to his staff. Mr. Bristol aimed not at a mob of agents, but a few highly trained, efficient men. He worked several years and succeeded in developing fourteen who were the apples of his eye. One day Richard A. McCurdy stepped in and appropriated practically the whole lot. He guaranteed salaries ranging anywhere from $250 to $1000 a month. Mr. Bristol found himself all but the sole representative of the Northwestern Mutual in New York, and had painfully to begin work all over again.

The Mutual and its rivals have wasted unnumbered thousands in this fashion. They would pay a man $1000, $2000, $3000, and $5000 flat to leave his com- pany, and liberal commissions in addition. Frequently such acquisitions would get this bonus and a year's guaranteed salary, produce little or no business, and then return to the old company. Nearly all of Mr. Bristol's agents, on the occasion described above, went back to him in a few months. The Big Three have frequently entered into pacts not to disturb each other's men, but usually have broken them. In 1900, for example, an agreement of this sort existed. In that year, however, the Equitable made a slight reduction in first year's commissions. The New York Life thought this a good opportunity to raid the Equitable's agency force. Vice-President Gage E. Tarbell retaliated in New York. He sent for R. J. Mix, the New York Life's leading agency director, and spent Sunday with him; on Monday morning Mr. Mix and some two hundred of the New York Life's New York representatives were carrying Equitable rate books. The New York Life replied by buying off, with flat bonuses and liberal advances, the larger part of the Equitable's staff in Buffalo.

The home offices have prodded this agency force in every possible manner. They have acquainted their men with the amount of new business expected each year, and have used all kinds of inducements, moral and material, in obtaining it. They have compensated agents in a bewildering variety of ways. They have paid commissions, salaries, bonuses, and prizes. When Hyde started the Equitable, first year's commissions did not usually exceed 10 per cent. of the first premium. He soon advanced that to 15, then to 25, then 35, and

then 50. In the last few years his rivals have thrown
aside all restraint. They have paid 50, 75, 80, and 90
per cent. of the first premium. The Mutual Life has
paid its New York agency ninety-six cents out of
every dollar collected in new premiums. Many smaller
companies have followed their example. Such minor
companies as the Home Life and the Manhattan have
managed their agency forces most extravagantly. The
United States Life, though most of its business is on
the deferred dividend basis, has absolutely no surplus;
it has used it all up in agents' commissions. Two years
ago the Washington Life became insolvent. The insurance department discovered that it had paid as high as
200 per cent. for new business. In recent years even
several of the Massachusetts companies, once among
the most conservative, have spent unwarrantably large
sums on the agency force. These commissions have
varied according to the particular policy written. The
New York managers have paid high for the contracts
which they especially desired to write. They have paid
low commissions on annual dividend policies, and high
on deferred. Again, they have graded these commissions
according to the length of the deferred dividend period.
They have paid higher commissions on ten-year than
five, higher on fifteen-year than ten, and highest of
all on twenty. In other words, they have paid the very

highest commission on the contracts which most unfavourably affected the policy-holder.

SUMMER OUTINGS, BONUSES, GOLD WATCHES, PUNCH BOWLS, AND CHESTS OF SILVER

Several years ago, also, they originated the bonus system. Under this they pay a larger compensation, provided a certain amount of business is obtained in a specified time. An agent, for example, may get 60 or 70 per cent. on all policies written. But if he turns in $100,-000 or $200,000 during the year, he will get, say, two dollars a thousand more on the entire annual business. This leads not only to extravagance, but to rebating—of which more presently. The New York Life has expended $500,000 in bonuses in a single year. It and the Equitable have also distributed large sums in prizes. The Equitable adorns its successful men with scarf-pins, watches, and diamond rings in recognition of duty well done. It also entertains them at enormous cost to the policy-holders. Last September, when the insurance excitement was at a white heat, the Equitable spent $50,000 fêting its agents at Manhattan Beach. The New York Life has spent as much as $125,000 on agents' conventions. It has its celebrated $100,000 and $200,000 clubs. Eligibility to the first depends on writing $100,000 of business in a single year; to the

second, $200,000. Each has its outing, but that of the
$200,000 club is quite a sumptuous affair. The members
bring their wives—at the policy-holders' expense, of
course; and the jollifications frequently extend through
five or six days. They hold forth at expensive hotels in
Put-in-Bay, Niagara Falls, Thousand Islands, Virginia
Hot Springs, and other noted resorts. Such occasions
usually end in a blaze of glory. An elaborate banquet
is held, speeches made, songs sung, and good things
passed around. Repeating watches, punch bowls, safety
razors, travelling bags, fountain pens, and chests of
silver—paid for by the widow and orphan—are distributed to the year's "biggest producers." Frequently
the high officers grace these banquets. A few years ago
singers were hired—again at the policy-holders' expense
—to discourse at a Waldorf-Astoria banquet a plain-
tive ballad especially composed in honour of John A.
McCall. Mr. McCall himself sat upon the platform.

PENSION AND DEATH BENEFITS AT POLICY-HOLDERS' EXPENSE

The New York Life not only pays its agents well,
but pensions them in their old age, and, in certain cases,
pays death benefits. It treats its agency directors with
especial liberality. It has some two hundred and twenty,
each drawing from $2000 to $6000 salary a year. Be-

sides this each gets $100 for each new agent secured. He also receives certain benefits if he remains with the company a certain time, and his widow receives a lump sum if he dies. In one year the New York Life has paid $259,000 to this pension fund. Agency directors get from $2000 to $10,000 if they die; inspectors of agencies, $10,000; and supervisors $7500. Under its celebrated Nylic system the New York Life also pensions all agents who reach a certain period of seniority after having done a certain amount of work.

The New York companies pay enormous amounts not only for work actually done, but for work not done at all.

They permit the agents to anticipate their earnings, to draw large amounts on commission account, to be paid back when the hoped-for policies are issued. They also permit the agents to draw largely in advance their renewal commissions. The Equitable, at the end of 1904, had thus advanced some $7,000,000. Certain agents had received advances amounting to $400,000, $600,000, and $850,000. The conservatively managed companies made such advances only on a limited scale. The Mutual Benefit, at the close of 1904, had lent only $71,000 to its agents; the Connecticut Mutual only $658. Ostensibly, advances are made that an agent may establish his business or extend it. If he has many policies on the books, all regularly paying premiums, he assigns his interest in these renewal commissions as security for loans. To a certain extent the system thus seems justified. Its weakness, however, consists in the enormous lapse rate. The agents who get the largest advances are usually the largest rebaters. They purchase, with advances, an immense amount of business that does not renew. Thus, to a great extent, even the ostensible security for the loans does not exist. In 1901 the Equitable Life calmly crossed $2,000,000 agents' advances off its books—money, that is, entirely uncollectable. Most state insurance departments no longer recognise these " advances " as valid assets. Single agents have left owing enormous sums, which have never been collected. A. G. Dickinson, the manager of the New York Life's South American department, resigned in 1888 owing $302,000, of which only $68,000 was ever obtained.

" ADVANCE MEN " AND LIFE-INSURANCE TRAMPS

The general agents, in their turn, have distributed these advances largely among their subordinates—the solicitors in the field. The new agent, especially, having no capital or other means of support, lives on " advances." He gets so much a week—$25 or $50—for several months, in the hope that he may write policies enough to pay back. In recent years almost any man could obtain employment on this basis from one of the three big companies. Consequently, thousands temporarily in hard luck have branched out as life-insurance solicitors. Some entered the business seriously; thousands, however, aimed merely at the salary. These have been technically known as " advance men." Others have referred to them as the " Bread Line." As long as the advances lasted they remained; when the patience of a particular company had been exhausted, they joined the ranks of another, still on " advances." A fine brood of life-insurance tramps has thus developed: men who oscillated from one company to another, living on " advances " and actually doing little or no work. Occasionally, the same man would draw " advances " from one company and turn such business as he got into another; more frequently, the same man would draw advances from more than one company. The same man has even drawn more than one advance from the same company. A few years ago the New York Life discovered that one man was drawing seven advances of $25 a week from seven different New York agencies under seven different names. Indeed, at times, it has almost seemed that the best man was not the one who wrote the most insurance, but the one who drew the most advances from the most companies at the same time. It is not insisted that this sort of thing has been encouraged; it is simply the abuse of the existing system.

LARGE TRAFFIC IN DECEPTIVE POLICIES

Probably no institutions devised by man have generated more liars and frauds than the New York life-insurance companies. The agents have lived largely upon the grossest misrepresentations. The companies have demanded only one qualification in agents—the ability to get business. They have not cared how they got it; and have tolerated, year in and year out, men of demonstrated dishonesty. Many agents have been extremely ignorant, and have not precisely realised the extent of their own deceptions. As far back as 1887 President Beers, of the New York Life, declared that 90 per cent. of life-insurance agents made " what people call misrepresentations," and he confessed his inability to change conditions. The agents have deliberately played upon the ignorance of the public. They have handled a product which few have understood. It is technical and deals in complicated figures. The agents have thus found it easy to deceive. They have gathered in everybody, from the tenement dweller to the captain of industry. One of the humours of the situation, indeed, has been the ease with which the life-insurance agent has gone into Wall Street and transformed the most aggressive bulls and bears into innocent lambs.

The agents have taken it for granted that the average policy-holder never reads his policy; and signs. applications without knowing what they mean. This assumption has usually been justified. The simplicity with which the average citizen purchases a $10,000 or $20,000 life-insurance policy without investigating its merits is part of the psychology of the trade. The agents have not facilitated his education; at best they have furnished bewildering arrays of comparative figures, " ratios," the attempted interpretation of which is sufficient to derange the average mind. In most cases the agent has been a particular friend, and has thus been depended upon to give fair treatment. His most obvious deception has been the " estimates " furnished upon Tontine and deferred dividend policies, already described in detail. He has also constantly sold these Tontines as endowments. The agent has repeatedly talked one policy and delivered another. There are many policy forms which sound alike, though radically different in character. There are, for example, twenty-year endowments, twenty-payment life policies, and ordinary life policies—all having twenty-year dividend periods. The first are the regulation endowments —payable to the insured after twenty years, or to the

beneficiaries if death occurs within that period. The
twenty-payment is the ordinary life policy payable in
twenty premiums; after twenty years, that is, the policy
is paid up. The face, however, is payable only to the
beneficiary at the death of the insured. The twenty-year
deferred dividend is a regular life policy, in which
the dividends are paid at the expiration of twenty
years.

The agents have sold twenty-payments as twenty-year
endowments; and twenty-year deferred dividend policies as twenty-payments. The insured, for example,
may have negotiated a regular twenty-year endowment
with a rival company. In steps a New York agent: " I
can give you this at a much lower rate," he says; and
quotes prices on a twenty-payment. To the lay mind the
things are so similar that he easily accomplishes the
deception. The agents have also found abundant opportunities in a certain so-called "instalment policy."
Under this, the beneficiary receives the death payment
not in one lump sum but in instalments. The premium
is less than that of an ordinary life. Many agents, however, have palmed them off as regular policies. They
used them especially in competition. "Look here!"
they would say; "I can give you the same policy as
the other fellow offers, though at greatly reduced
rates," and then they would furnish the figures for

instalment policies. The widow, after the insured dies, is the first to discover the imposition.

"GOLD BONDS," "CONSOLS," AND "DEBENTURES"

The agents, however, have not found opportunities enough in the orthodox forms. They have inspired the invention of numerous picturesque contracts. Under their houndings the actuary's life has become a burden. In reality, there are only three forms of life insurance: the regular life policy, payable at death; the endowment, payable to the beneficiary at death and to the insured provided he survives a stipulated period; and the term policy, which insures a man, not for life, but for a certain period, ten, fifteen, or twenty years. There are various ways of paying for these policies, and of distributing the dividends; but essentially these are the only three possible forms. For thirty years the actuaries have utilised all their ingenuity in twisting them into something new. The Equitable and the Mutual have had upon their market between two and three hundred forms of policy; all merely changes rung upon these three original types. They have constantly harped upon the "investment idea." "Make the Mutual Life your savings bank," has become the war cry. They have given the semblance of investment frequently by combining one form of policy with another.

One thing the policy-holder can always depend upon, however: he pays for everything he gets. The price rests upon certain scientific principles; no company can disregard them without disaster. What one company offers another can offer; and any policy that contains unusual opportunities also carries a premium that completely pays for them. All modern novelties are simply old forms of life insurance under new names—and usually at greatly increased prices.

In recent years, for example, the New York companies have gone daft over " gold bonds," " consols," and " debentures." They found that the public had tired of life insurance, and so dropped this business largely in favour of the " gold bond." " I don't want any life insurance; I've got more than I can carry now," you tell the agent. " But, my dear sir, this is not life insurance, this is a new issue of bonds—an investment for yourself," he replies. He has the thing pretty thoroughly disguised. You do not sign an " application " for insurance, but a " subscription." You do not become a policy-holder, but a " subscriber." You do not pay a premium, but an " instalment." An annuity becomes a " guaranteed interest "; a paid-up policy, an " extension of the bond "; a death payment, a " mortuary return." In the document you receive, the word " life insurance " is not mentioned once. It is a

very expensive affair, printed in gold leaf, and, in the
case of the New York Life, gorgeously surrounded
by the coloured flags of all nations. After paying for
twenty years you obtain the Equitable's bond for, say,
$10,000 running for twenty years at 5 per cent. inter-
est and then redeemed. If you die before the twenty
years expire, your widow gets $20,000 or a " gold
bond " for that amount. Actually, the bond contract
is simply a twenty-year endowment policy. Instead of
getting your $10,000 in cash, as under an ordinary
endowment, the company keeps the principal, pays an
annuity for twenty years, and then pays the full
amount. The deception consists in the fact that the
Equitable advertises this as a *5 per cent.* gold bond. It
does not pay 5 per cent. in fact. The Equitable charges
you an " instalment " (*i. e.,* premium) so large that it
reduces the income to two-and-a-half, or three. It
charges for a $10,000 twenty-year gold endowment
bond at age forty, $706. Its price for regular twenty-
year endowment for $13,000 is precisely the same. That
is, if you buy a gold bond, instead of a regular endowment, you pay for a $13,000 policy and get one for
only $10,000. In other words, you pay a *large premium*
on your bond, which reduces the investment rate. You
get 5 per cent. on $10,000, when you should get 5 per
cent. on $13,000. Thus, in this case, your gold bond

actually yields 3 per cent. instead of 5. The Equitable, the New York Life, and the Mutual have gulled thousands of capitalists by this transparent trick. Eminent lawyers have examined the gold bond and recommended it as an investment, never once detecting the carefully concealed Ethiopian.

LIFE INSURANCE "FREE OF COST"

The New York companies have also largely purveyed the "return premium policy." Under this, all your premiums, in addition to the face of the policy, are returned at death. This is "life insurance free of cost," as one New York Equitable agent had the temerity to advertise it. This policy has been brought forth in emergencies. The agents used it to prove finally that they could better any policy written by other companies. The prospective insurant invariably stood aghast. "What! insure my life; then, if I die, pay the policy and return all the premiums I have paid?" Yet it is the simplest thing in the world. The company could afford to return not only all your premiums, but could throw in a steam yacht and give you a house on Fifth Avenue. It exacts only one condition in all three cases: and that is that you pay a premium large enough to insure the risk carried. For even on the "return premium" policy you could not beat the company. On such contracts it always charged two premiums; though they were lumped together in the payment. One covered the cost of the insurance itself; the other the cost of insuring the return of the premiums. The premium charged on such policies, that is, is higher than the ordinary kind. In the old days the New York Life issued a five-year dividend policy. It guaranteed, that is, a dividend, the amount stated in the policy, at the end of five years. It simply charged each year the full premium for the policy, and then added another premium which insured the amount agreed to be returned as a "dividend." "Aha!" declares some especially shrewd policy-holder, thinking he detects the weak spot in the "return premium" policy. "It is not life insurance free of cost, because you don't return the interest on the premiums." The agent can meet even this objection. He adds another little premium—the third—large enough to insure the repayment of the interest.

REBATES: LIFE INSURANCE "ROUNDERS"

The agents have practised discrimination by the wholesale grant of rebates. Rebating, it may be explained, is the agent's habit of dividing his first year's commission with the prospective insurant. Frequently, he gives more—sometimes 80 or 90 per cent., or the whole of the first premium. As far back as 1879, as we have learned, rebating had become general; in 1887 President Beers, of the New York Life, declared that it was the " curse of the business." From the first the managements themselves have encouraged it. At the Beers investigation in 1887 it developed that not only the agents, but the company itself, gave rebates. They promised reductions on renewals; and, in many instances, the home office accepted these reduced premiums in full payment. Occasionally, it divided the expense of rebating with the agent. Nowadays, a large policy-holder who pays the full first year's premium is looked upon as an innocent.

The practice is vicious from various standpoints. It discriminates between policy-holders, especially between the rich and the poor. As a rule the smaller policy-holders get no rebate; it is an inducement especially offered for " big men." In other words, the poor pay big prices for their insurance, the rich small. If your premium is $25 a year, you pay the full price; if it is $200, you can usually get anywhere from 50 to 90 per cent. off. Discrimination exists not only between the rebated and the unrebated, but between the rebated themselves. The agents throw off just as much, or just as little, as the occasion requires. They sell policies precisely as the old Baxter Street " puller-in " used to sell clothes: that is, they get as much as they can. The marketing of life-insurance policies has largely degenerated into barter. Rather than not deliver the big policy, the agent will give back the whole first year's premium.

Rebating is vicious on other grounds. It brings an enormous amount of shifty business, and is largely responsible for the prevailing lapse rate. Many, because of the first year's rebate, take larger policies than they can afford, and drop them the second year. Again, it has developed a brood of life-insurance "rounders." A few years ago Harlem flat owners attracted tenants by giving three or four months' rent free. As a consequence, many families kept moving from flat to flat, spending three months in each, and thus living without paying any rent at all. Similarly, many ingenious persons have obtained life insurance all but "free of cost." This year, for example, you take a $10,000 policy in the Equitable, at 75 or 80 or 90 per cent. discount. Instead of paying your second premium you take next year a policy in the Mutual— also at a big discount. The year after that you take the same policy in the New York Life. The fourth year you come back to the Equitable, and repeat the performance indefinitely.

Occasionally, a rebated policy-holder becomes physically impaired;—what is known as a bad risk. Then

he sticks in the company into which he was last rebated.
A sick man always hungers for life insurance. A man
who ordinarily could afford a $10,000 policy takes one
for $100,000 at 90 per cent. off. If he falls sick, his
relatives and friends gladly pay the few remaining
premiums, and his widow, at death, pockets a neat
$100,000. This is paid, of course, out of the funds of
the unrebated policy-holders. Rebating, in other words,
promotes " adverse selection "; that is, brings into the
company unhealthy lives and thus increases the death
rate. The Big Three write an enormous new annual
business, but do not increase in size proportionately.
The explanation is that much of the business is obtained
by rebates, and does not renew. " How's business? " a
high official of a New York company asked a rival a
few years ago. " Same old Hell," he replied, referring
to conditions described above.

PRESENTS FOR POLICY-HOLDERS' WIVES

The New York companies loudly assert that they
have warred on the rebaters for years. Mr. Gage E.
Tarbell declared, at the recent New York investigation,
that in spite of all his efforts at reform, life-insurance
policies could be bought, at certain times of the year,
for 10 cents on the dollar. A law exists in New York
State prohibiting rebates; but the agents have ingen-

iously circumvented it. They take notes in payment for the larger part of the premium, and make no attempt to collec them. They make presents to the new policy-holder's wife—a silk dress, a watch, a boa. Farmers pay the larger part of their first premium in potatoes; railroad officials in passes; newspaper editors in advertisements. The agents give free fire or casualty insurance policies.

Rebaters demoralise the field for the conscientious, hard-working agent. The New York companies have had certain star producers—"executive specials." These gentlemen make a specialty of large risks. They spurn the little $2000 or $5000 man, and smoke out the $100,000, $500,000, perhaps the $1,000,000 policy-holder. They are attached to no office, but have roving commissions to travel from town to town. They live on "advances" in the most expensive fashion. At night they can frequently be found, in evening clothes, in the lobbies of certain high-priced hotels. They entertain lavishly; edge their way into the clubs; frequently even achieve some standing in "society." They enter a field which a careful general agent has perhaps cultivated for years. They write policies, making rebates right and left. Exhausting one town, they drop it and repeat the same performance elsewhere. After their departure the home agent finds it practically impossible to do business. The cream has been skimmed, and the public educated, by the few weeks' visit of the "executive special," to demand policies at bargain prices.

The companies are alone responsible for these practices. They themselves encourage rebating. They give away business because they have a mania for a big annual showing. Mr. George T. Wilson, an Equitable vice-president, has frankly explained the root of the evil. Rebating, he declared, at the recent New York investigation, is "an American product devised for home consumption." He openly admitted that the reason the agents gave back so much of the premium was because "they had it to give." That is, rebating is explained, above all, by the high commissions, bonuses, and advances paid in New York. If an agent gets only 25 per cent. of the first premium, he cannot afford to rebate, because there will be little left for himself. If he gets 75 or 90 per cent., he can divide with the policy-holder and still have something. Nor are the agents dependent upon their commissions for livelihoods. At any time they can dip into the policy-holders' dividends and take out thousands in the form of "advances." 'Again, the prevailing bonus and prize system causes rebating. The agent who writes $1,000,000 in a year, for example, may be entitled to a cash prize of $2000. In the latter part of December he may need $50,000 to make his quota. The premiums on this are perhaps $1500 less than half of what the agent must turn in to the company. He therefore corrals an acquaintance, gets him examined, and even though the agent pays the whole premium himself, pockets a profit of nearly $1500.

CAREER OF ONE SAMUEL DINKELSPIEL

New York methods can perhaps be best illustrated by describing the actual life-insurance career of one agent of continental reputation. Twenty years ago the New York Life's leading man was one Samuel Dinkelspiel. President Beers described him as his "lightning solicitor"; Rufus W. Weeks, the New York Life's actuary, declared on the witness stand that he regarded him as a "valuable man for the company." There were three Dinkelspiels: one in the New York Life and one in the Equitable, both of whom stood pre-eminent in the "profession." The third brother, located at New Orleans, was popularly differentiated as the "good Dinkelspiel." "Sam" Dinkelspiel, the New York Life man, was the flower of the family. He made his first appearance as a New York agent in Louisville, in the late '70's. Here he became involved in a disgraceful escapade; some said forgery; President Beers, a " woman scrape." At least he found it convenient to change his name to Lewis and depart for Canada. He represented the New York Life in Montreal for several years under this assumed name. One day the New York's general agent at Montreal, Mr. Burke, appeared in President Beers' New York office. His anxiety over Dinkelspiel, said Burke, kept him walking the floor nights. His methods, he declared, were outrageous; he wrote business by the grossest misrepresentation and constantly brought the New York Life into disrepute. Mr. Burke declared that he lived in daily terror lest Dinkelspiel do something especially serious for which the home office would hold himself responsible. He demanded the man's dismissal; President Beers acceded. Dinkelspiel, resuming his own name, then came to New York. He consorted with many of the worst people in town, spent a large part of his time at the race tracks, and had an irresistible fondness for poker. He found an opening in the United States Life. He obtained liberal advances and turned in a large amount of business of a certain kind.

He worked three or four years and then left, his financial relations with the company considerably involved. One day a dilapidated creature appeared in the

New York Life office. It was Dinkelspiel. He told President Beers that he had lost $4000 at cards and asked for "advances" to pay the debt. He could get no more money from the United States Life, he plaintively declared. President Beers gave him money and let him loose on the community. He achieved phenomenal success. President Beers gave him hundreds of thousands in advances; at one time Dinkelspiel drew as much as $30,000 a month. With this he travelled all over the country, making a specialty of rich men. He entrapped them by the scores. His like has never been known. He seemed possessed of some hypnotic influence. He could enter a millionaire's office unintroduced, talk a few moments, and go out with a $5000 check to cover the first premium. He insured such men as John V. Farwell of Chicago, E. J. Berwind, Walter Gurnee, Percy R. Pyne, of New York, and James Stillman, president of the National—Standard Oil—City Bank. Usually these same millionaires appeared in President Beers' office a few months after obtaining their policies, threatening lawsuits against the New York Life. For Dinkelspiel obtained his business by making huge rebates and promises, the audacity of which was little short of genius. He did not hesitate to put these promises in writing. He would offer a man a trusteeship in the New York Life, provided he took out a large

amount of insurance; he would promise him commissions not only on his own policy, but upon all policies
written in his section. Would he rebate? He would
make a contract, giving the man 50 per cent. off this
year, 15 the next, 10 the next, and so on. Checks were
sent to the home office, with Dinkelspiel's rebates deducted, and accepted in full payment. He insured one
man for $50,000, telling him that in fifteen years he
could exchange it for a $200,000 paid-up policy. He
promised a Boston man half the commission, on not
only his own policy, but on all others written in that
city. He reported to the home office hundreds of policies
which were never taken. One month he claimed to have
written $1,100,000 of new insurance. Of this, only
$100,000 was actually paid for. In spite of all this he
maintained his hold on the New York Life. Once, en-
raged because another agent had crossed his path,
Dinkelspiel threatened to resign; the New York Life
gave him $8000 to soothe his feelings. At another
time he and his brother, William Dinkelspiel, of the
Equitable, lost $50,000 in one day at the Saratoga
race track. President Beers admitted that the New
York Life paid $20,000 of this, and added that he
" had been informed that the Equitable paid the remaining $30,000." Mr. Beers rather chuckled because
the Equitable had made good the larger share. All these

facts about Dinkelspiel were laid before the trustees of the New York Life in 1887; and their answer was to continue him in their employ. When he left, two or three years later, he owed the policy-holders $348,000.

In the preceding articles have been detailed the causes of the recent life-insurance upheaval. The explanation, it is clear, strikes deeper than the popular imagination has supposed. One-hundred-thousand-dollar French balls, the control of an enormous property by a reckless spendthrift, even the struggle of selfish Wall Street interests for supremacy—these things do not explain the present crisis. They merely happened to be the particular incidents through which the actual facts became public property.

The actual disease, however, had been long seated. The personalities of Hyde and Alexander, picturesque and interesting as they may have been, were not the real issues. Whether this or that particular financial clique should control the Equitable, the Mutual, and the New York Life—that, after all, was not the main point; but whether a thirty years' Saturnalia, in which the very life-insurance idea itself had been prostituted, should end.

The real theme, in these articles, has been the rise and downfall of one of the greatest of American institutions. It has been shown that life insurance, though its principles had been theoretically worked out in England, was first reduced to honest and successful practice on a large scale in the United States. Elizur Wright, already distinguished as an Abolitionist, found the system in England the cover for the grossest frauds. His mathematical genius at once detected the cause; his moral enthusiasm inspired him to the long and thankless task of reforming it. By his legal reserve law he made certain the absolute solvency of life-insurance companies. By his non-forfeiture laws he made life insurance fair. Because of these two principles American life-insurance companies received a great popular impetus and became a national force making for solidity and good citizenship.

We have then discovered how, after Wright had accomplished this great task, Henry B. Hyde, by founding the Equitable, proceeded largely to destroy the structure. He added to life insurance a gambling device long discredited in Europe, which, under various names, Tontine and deferred dividend, became its prevailing idea. Instead of paying " dividends " annually, or annually returning to the policy-holder his over-payment, Hyde accumulated such overpayments, with the values of lapsing members, in a huge fund which he called surplus. Ostensibly, he proposed to divide this, after the expiration of twenty years, among all members who had paid their premiums regularly and still lived. He entered into no written contract to do this, however. In fact, he distributed a considerable part of this fund among his agents in the form of commissions and among himself and his favoured trustees in the form of plunder. He and his rivals who adopted the ideas used this fund in paying themselves enormous salaries, in corrupting the legislatures and the press, in building up large financial institutions for their own advantage and at the policy-holder's expense, and in engaging in certain forms of Wall Street speculation. At the end of long deferred dividend periods they returned to the deluded policy-holders such portion of this Tontine or deferred dividend fund as they had not thus wasted or stolen. They were able to perpetrate this fraud because they handled a produce which the average citizen did not understand, and upon which it was easy to mislead him. They did it by making the grossest misrepresentations about Tontine profits; and by engaging, by the use of that very Tontine fund, a huge army of agents who have spread broadcast these falsehoods. Such, in brief, is the story of a great financial hoax which must inevitably take its place in history side by side with the Mississippi Scheme and the South Sea Bubble.

Is the end yet? Much, indeed, has been accomplished. Above all, the laws passed as a result of the New York investigation absolutely prohibit deferred dividend policies. Thus they remove that opportunity for plunder which has corrupted so many men. They also prohibit subsidiary banks and trust companies, investments in stocks, and participation in speculative syndicates by trustees and directors; and demand publicity concerning salaries and other details. They attempt also to limit agents' commissions and the cost of new business. But the greatest evil they do not, and cannot, touch. That is the control of these enormous institutions by dishonest men. There can be no complete reform, whatever laws are passed, so long as the men who enforce them are untrustworthy. In the New York Life and the Mutual the leading trustees, under whose control all the abuses described above have developed and flourished, are still in control. In the Mutual Life men who have taken profits in underwriting syndicates at their policy-holders' expense still manage its finances. In the New York Life men who have tolerated falsification of records and the wildest agency extravagance have received a new lease of power. That there have been other exposures of insurance dishonesty has been shown in the foregoing articles. In 1870 the Superintendent of Insurance uncovered much dishonesty in the Mutual

Life. The Mutual Life bought him up and succeeded in suppressing the official document which described its shortcomings. In 1877 and in 1885 the true nature of the Equitable was partly laid bare; but the Equitable succeeded also in suppressing the facts. The last three chief executive officers of the New York Life have retired from office in disgrace: Pliny Freeman in 1863, William H. Beers in 1891, and John A. McCall in 1905. Whether the present disclosures will end in lasting reform, or whether the previous experience will be repeated, depends largely on whether the policy-holders take charge of their own property and cast out the men whose carelessness and dishonesty have been demonstrated.

THE END